I0391166

Color The Psalms

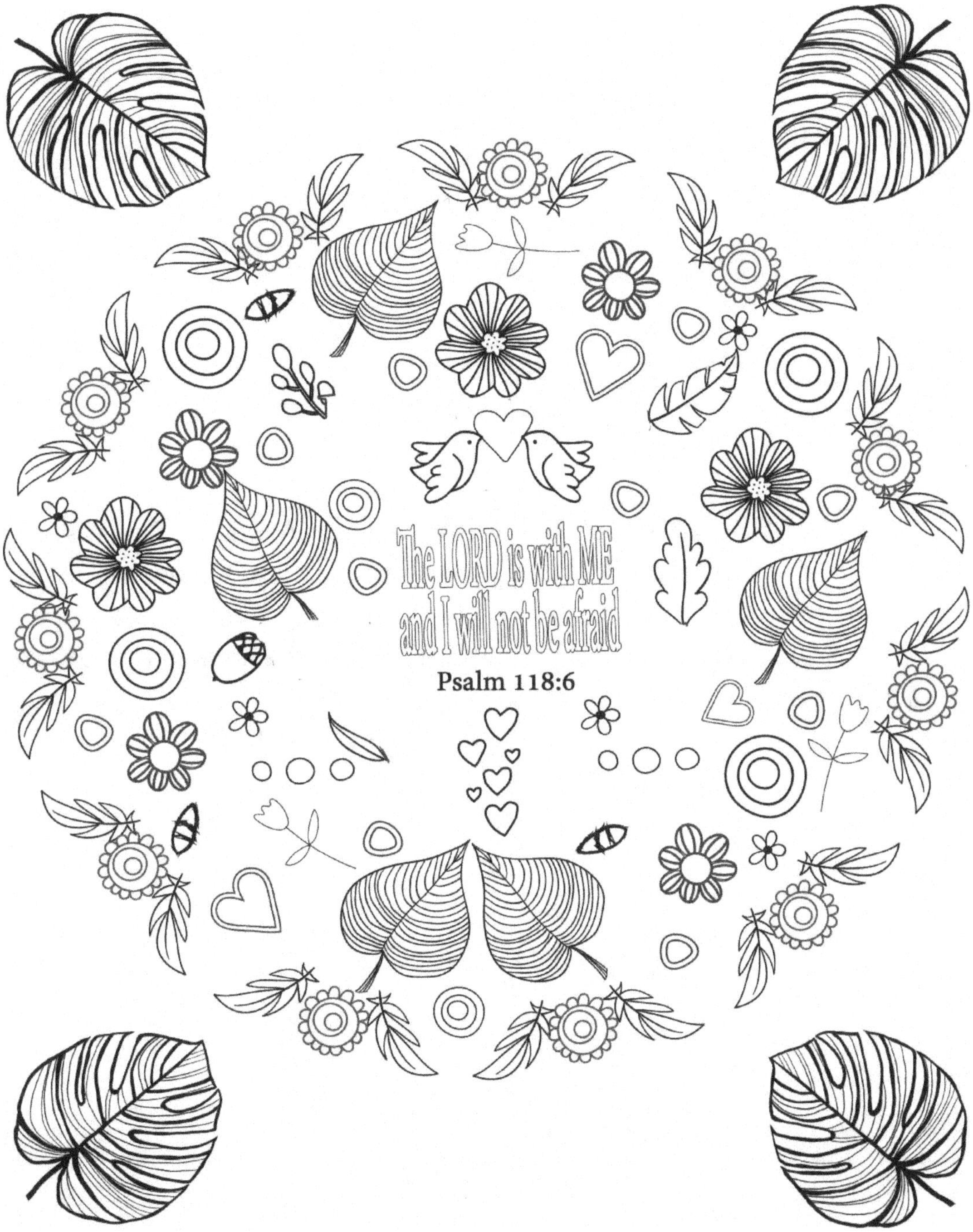

The LORD is with ME
and I will not be afraid

Psalm 118:6

Coloring Book With Bible Inspirations for Adults

Copyright 2016 'Coloring With The Lord' All Rights Reserved.
This book or any part of it may not be used
in any matter whatsoever without the express written permission
of the publisher except for the use of brief quotations in a book review

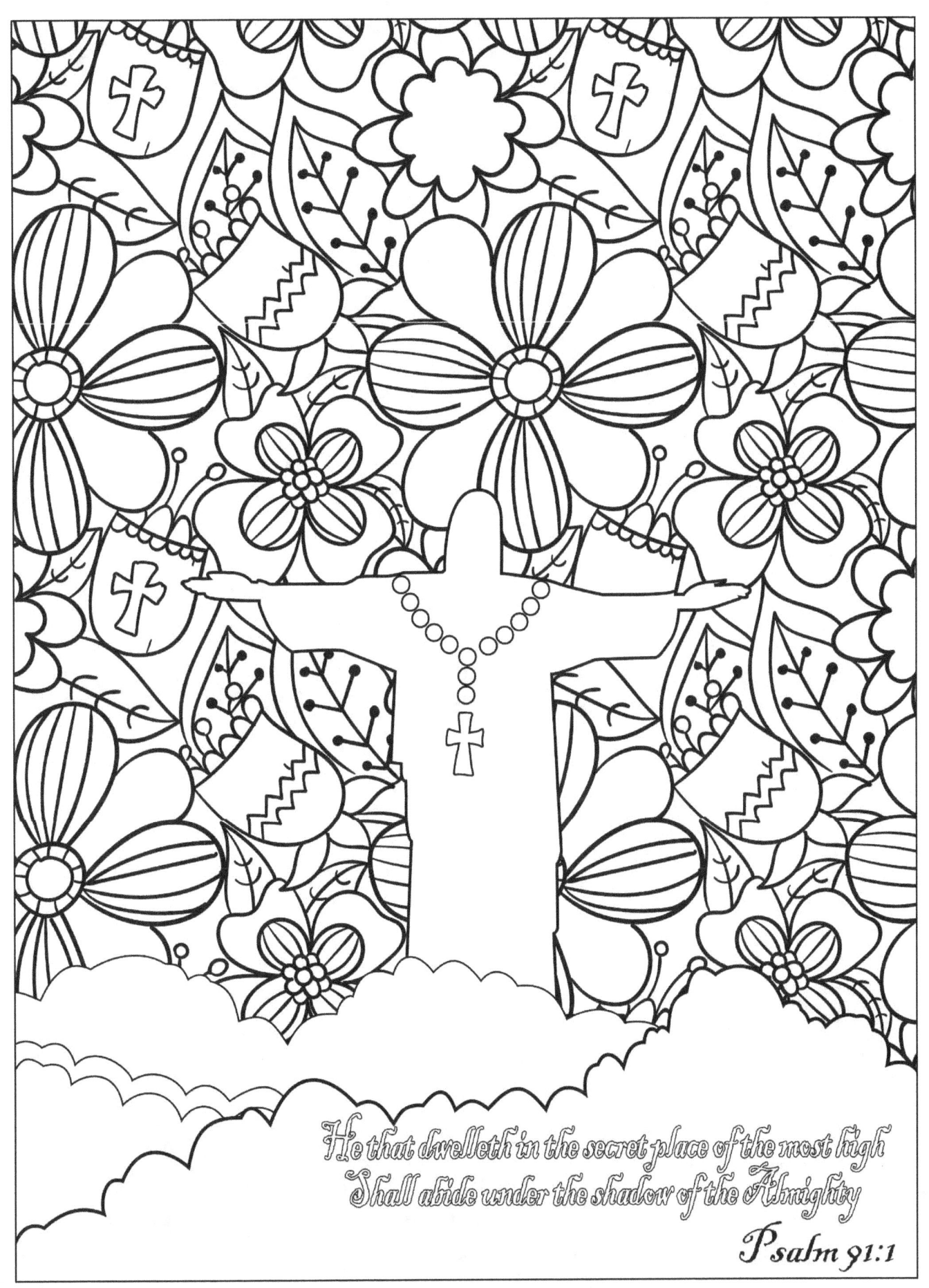

He that dwelleth in the secret place of the most high
Shall abide under the shadow of the Almighty

Psalm 91:1

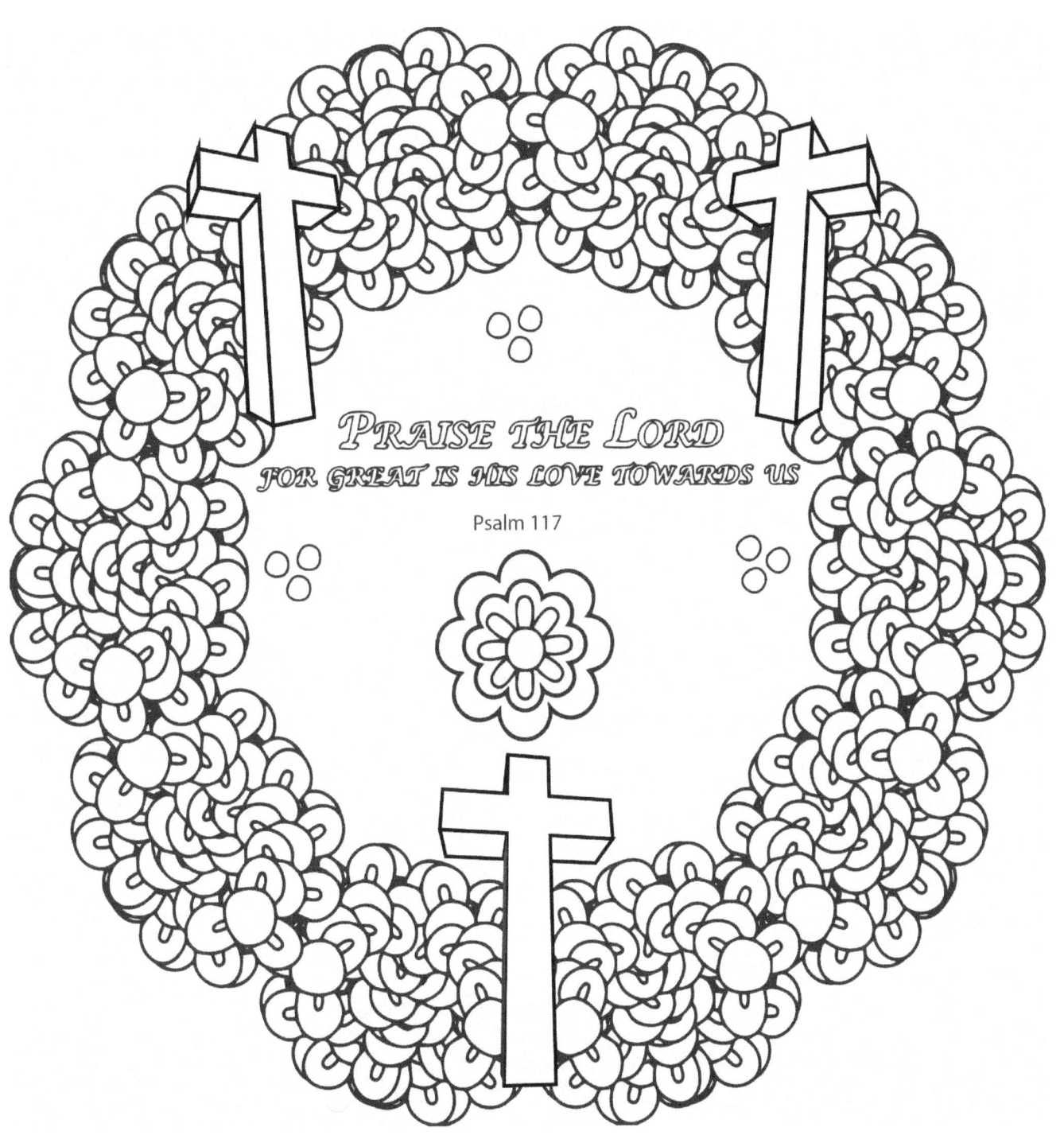

PRAISE THE LORD
FOR GREAT IS HIS LOVE TOWARDS US

Psalm 117

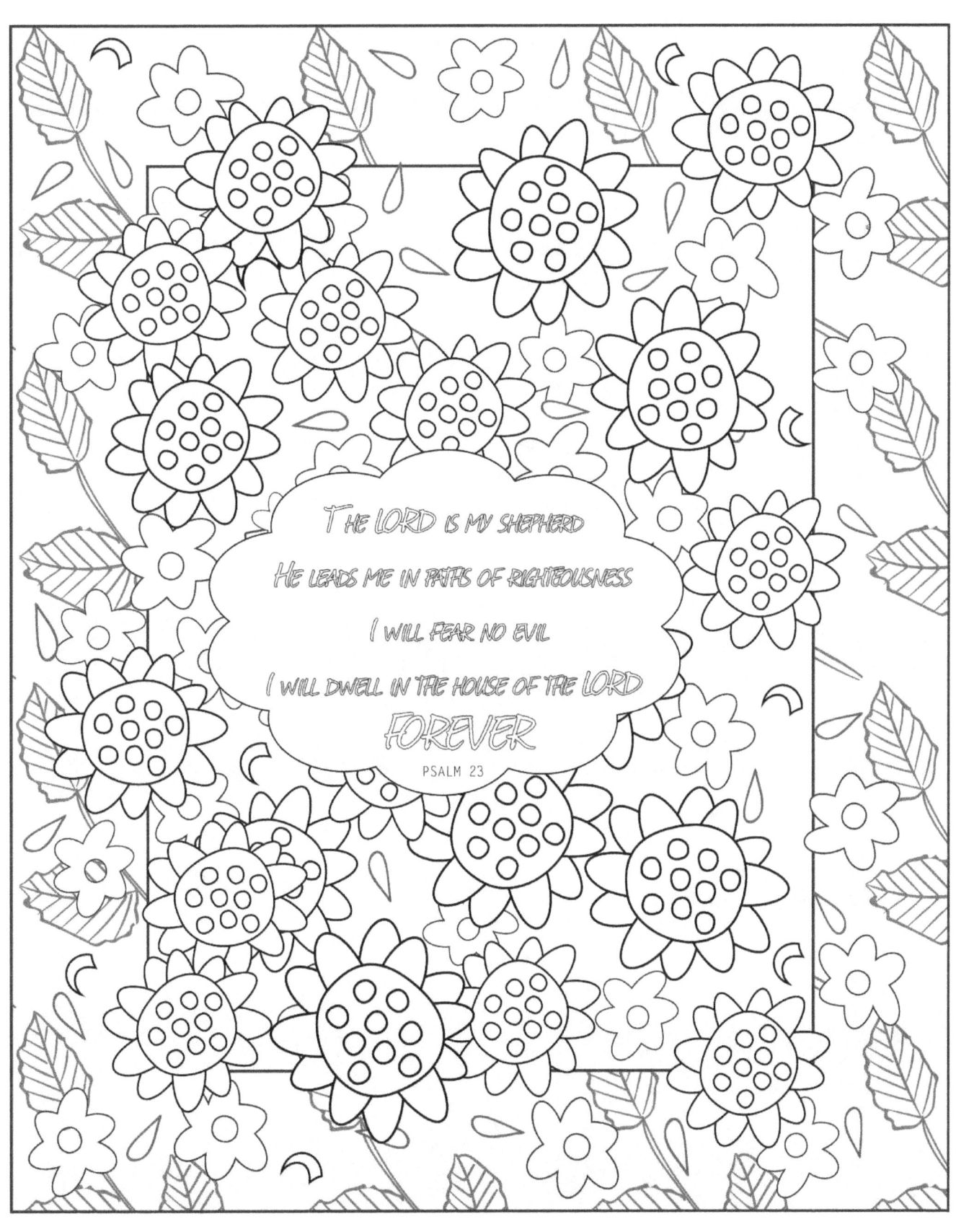

The LORD is my shepherd

He leads me in paths of righteousness

I will fear no evil

I will dwell in the house of the LORD

FOREVER

PSALM 23

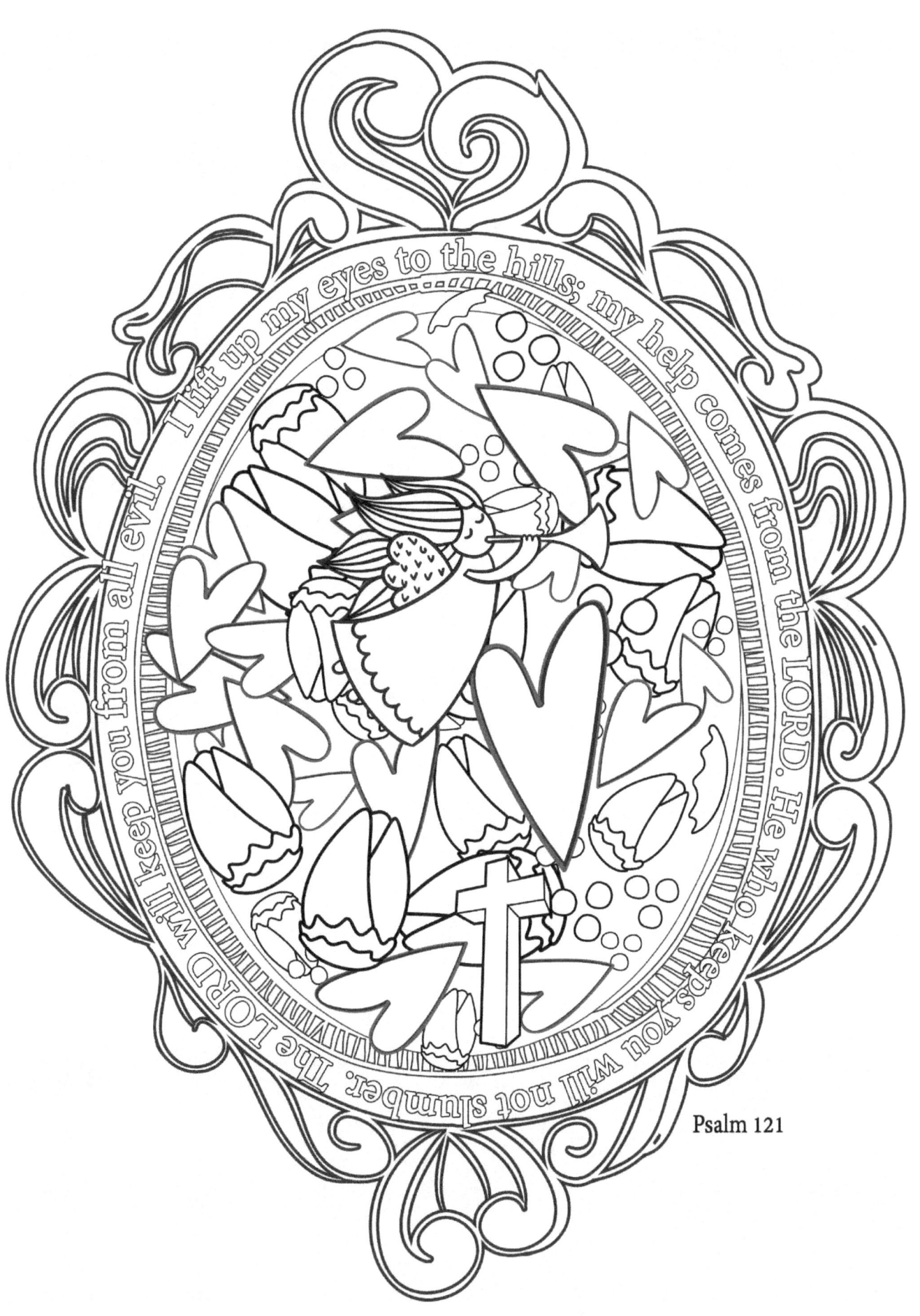

Psalm 121

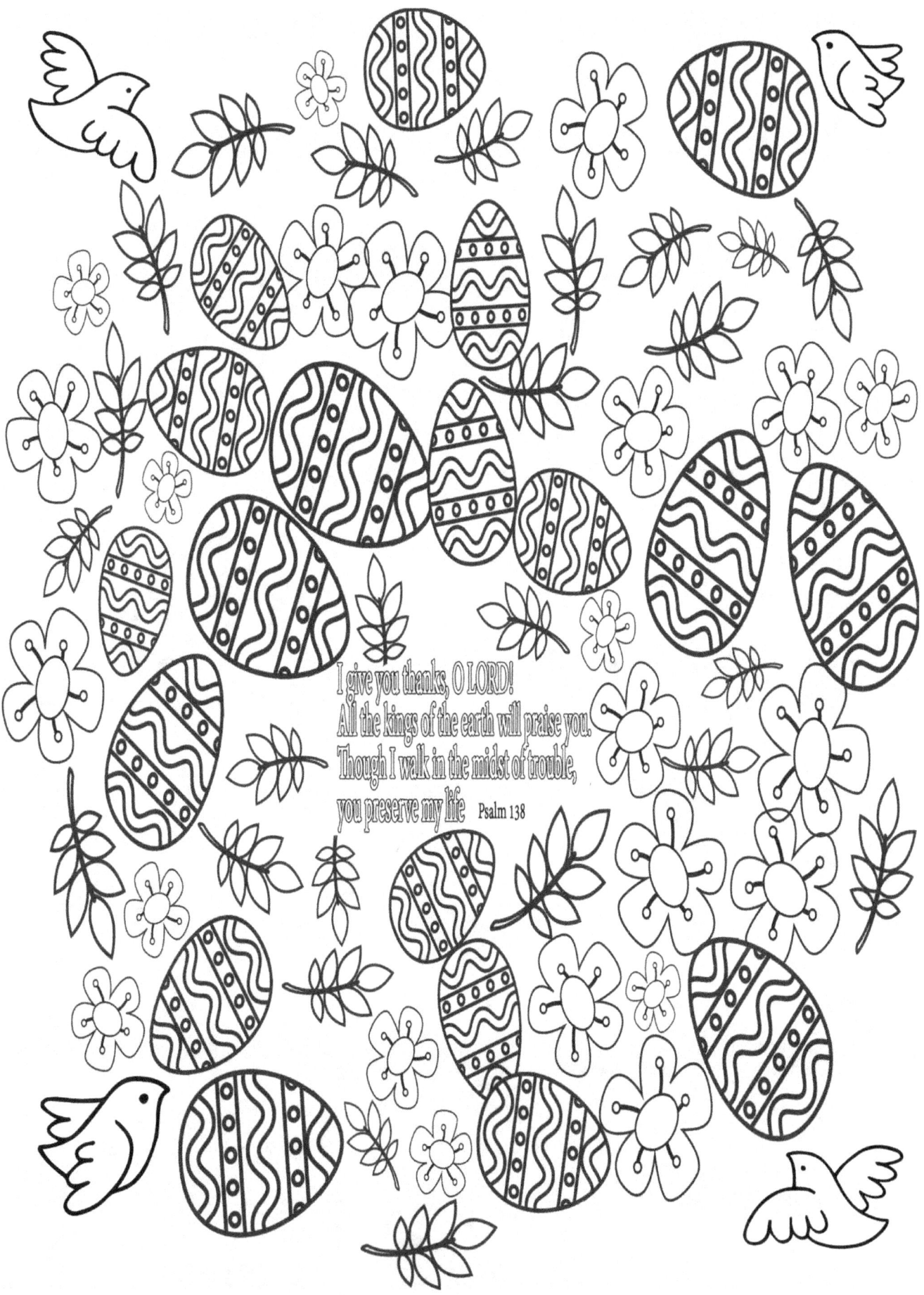

I give you thanks, O LORD!
All the kings of the earth will praise you.
Though I walk in the midst of trouble,
you preserve my life   Psalm 138

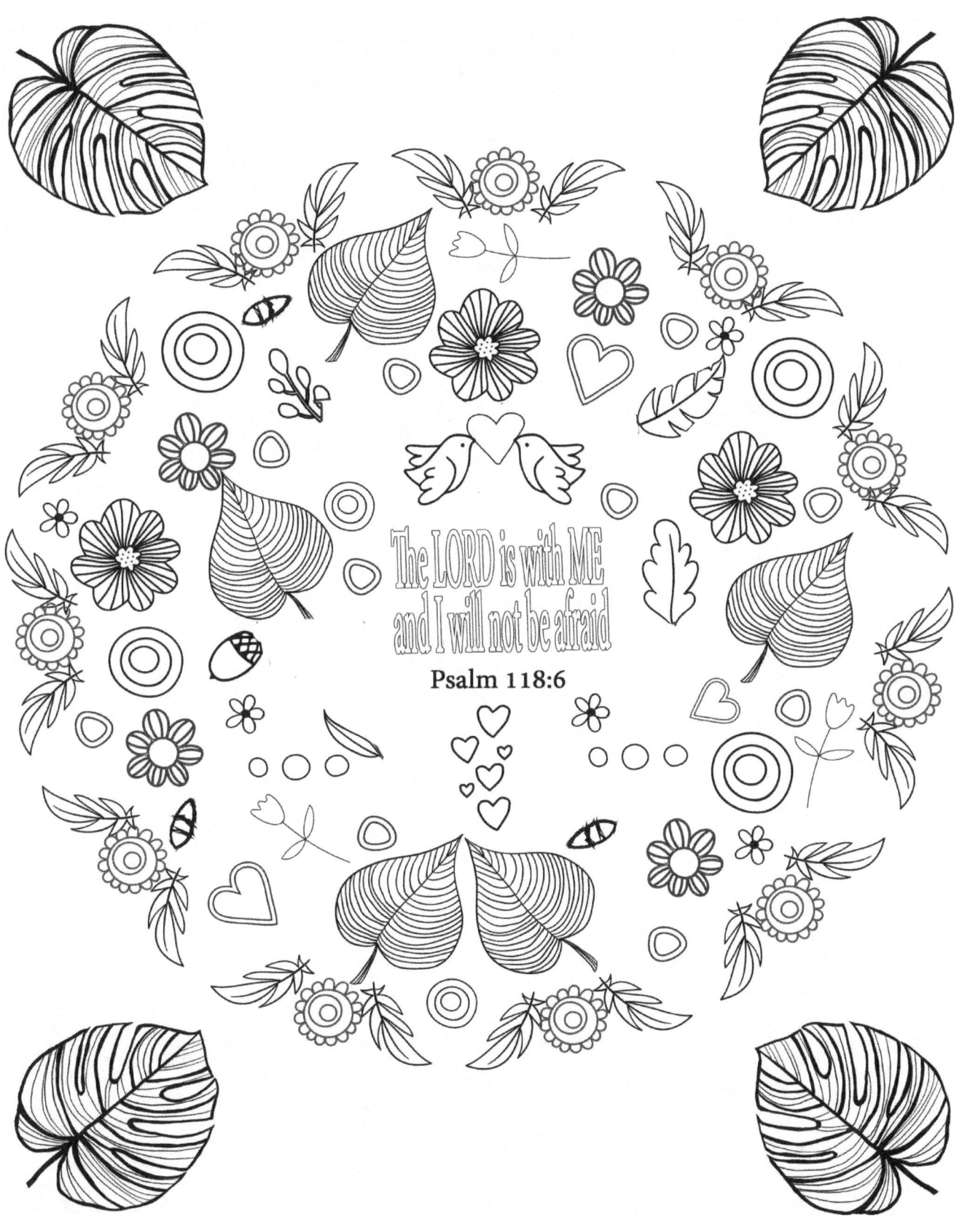

The LORD is with ME and I will not be afraid

Psalm 118:6

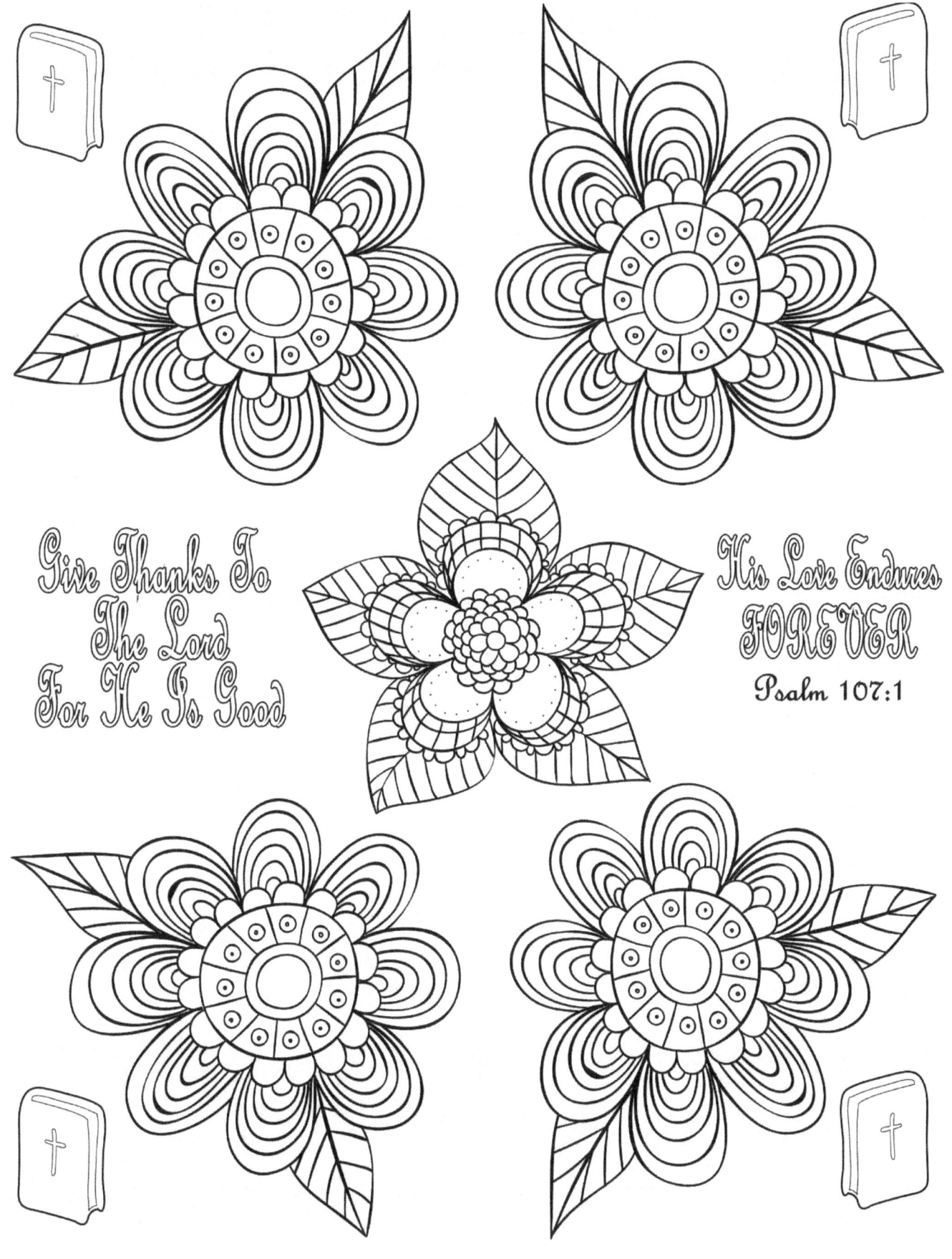

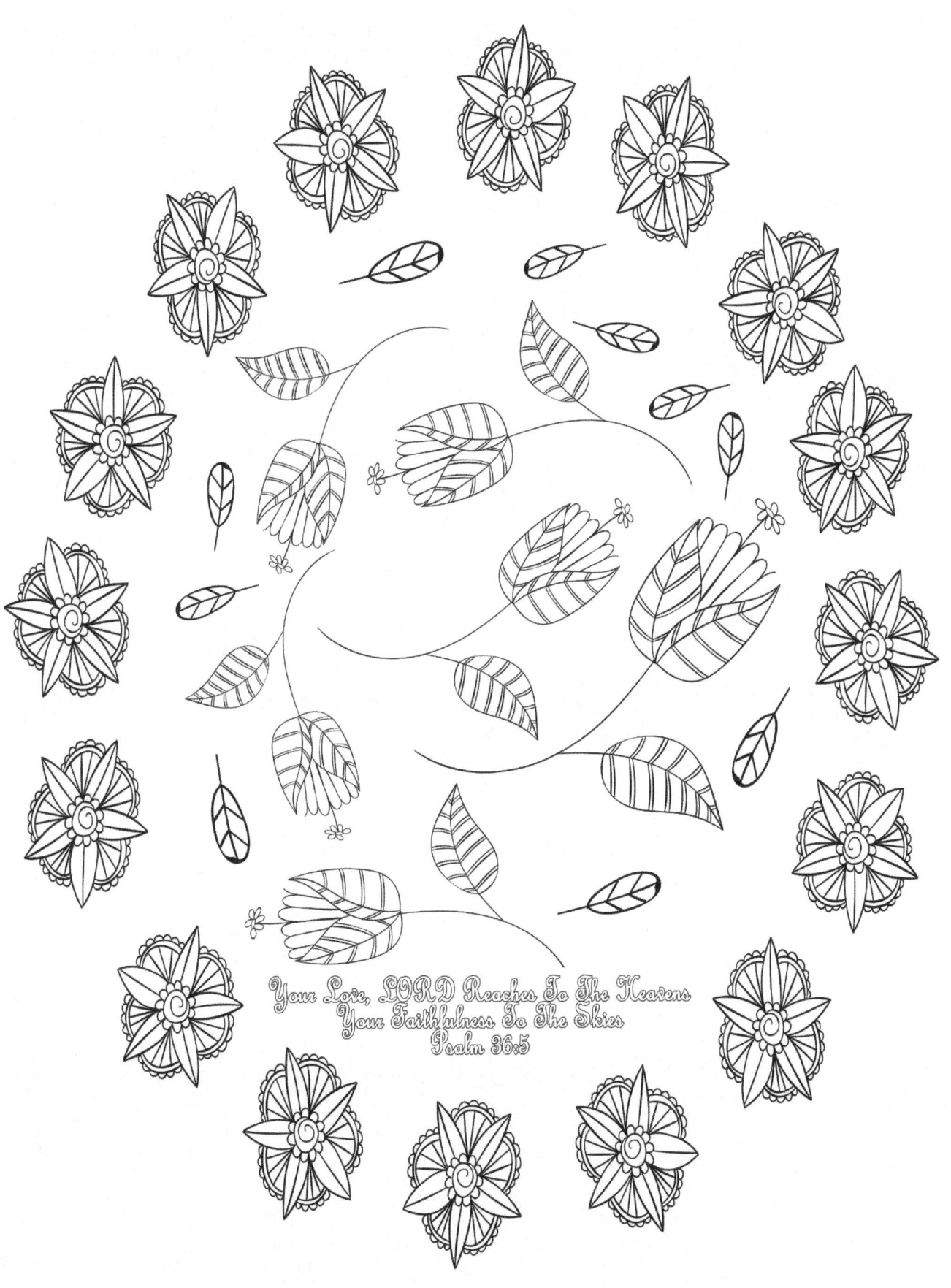

Your Love, LORD Reaches To The Heavens
Your Faithfulness To The Skies
Psalm 36:5

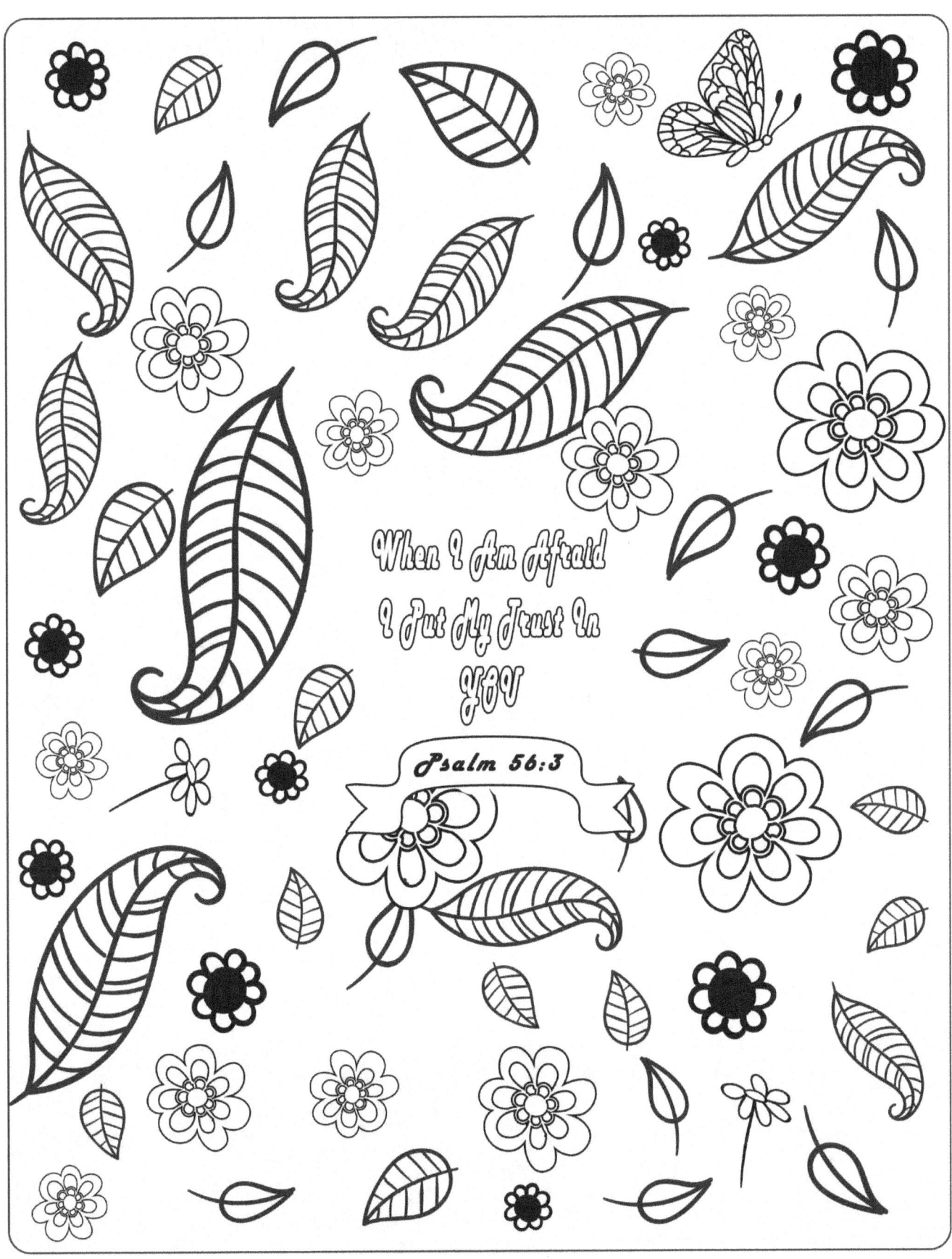

When I Am Afraid
I Put My Trust In
YOU

Psalm 56:3

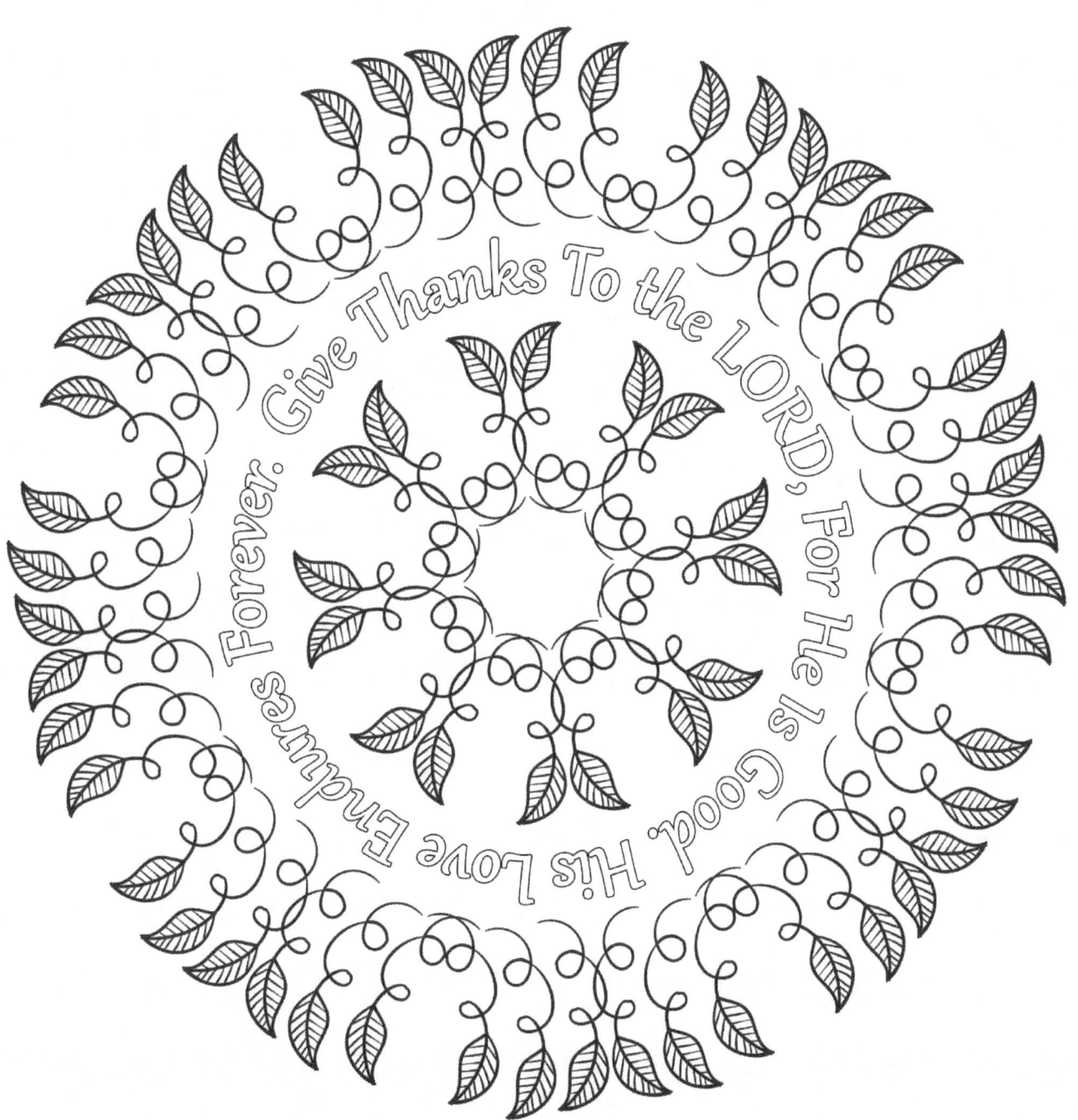

Give Thanks To the LORD, For He Is Good, His Love Endures Forever.

Psalm 136:1

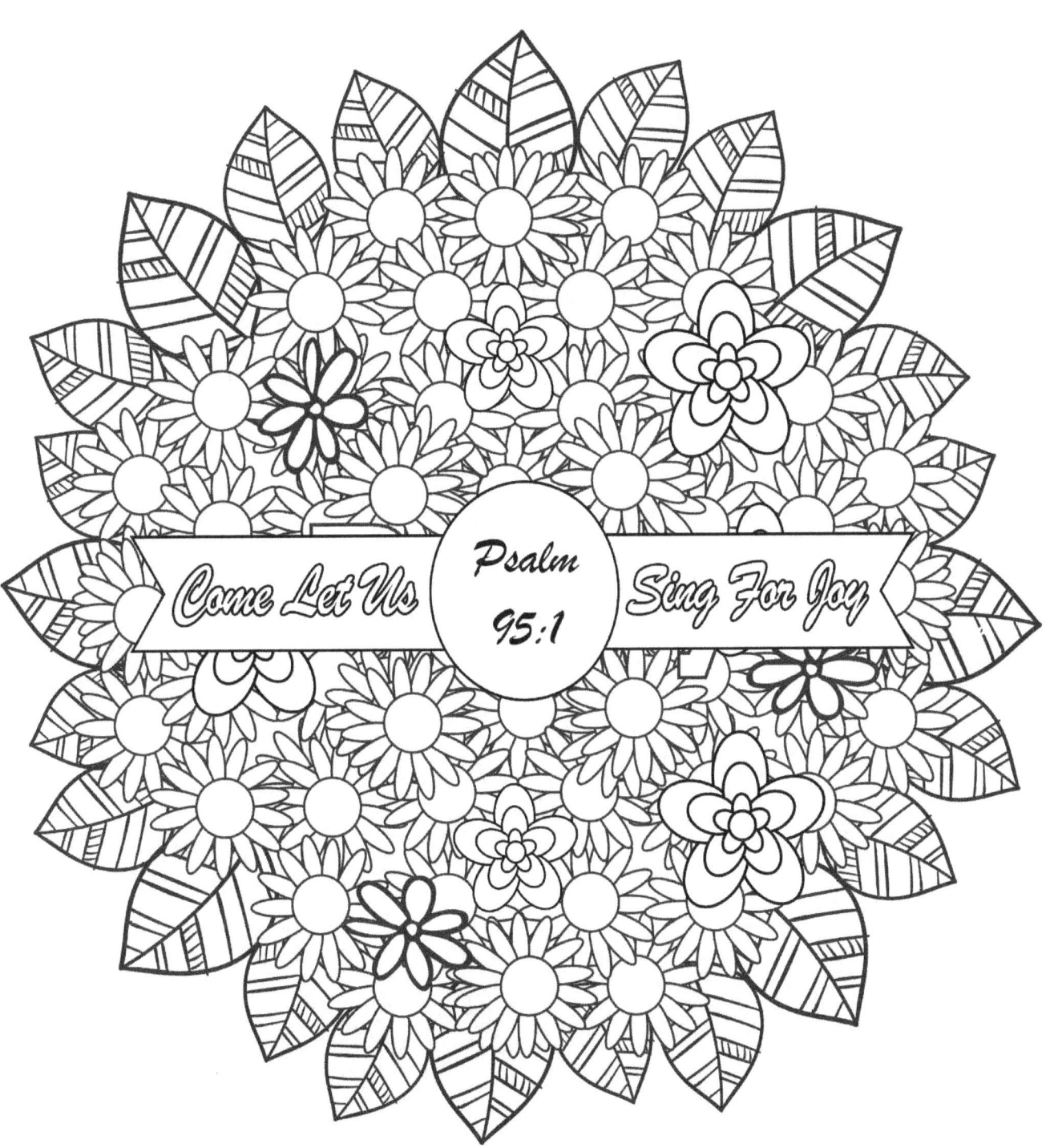

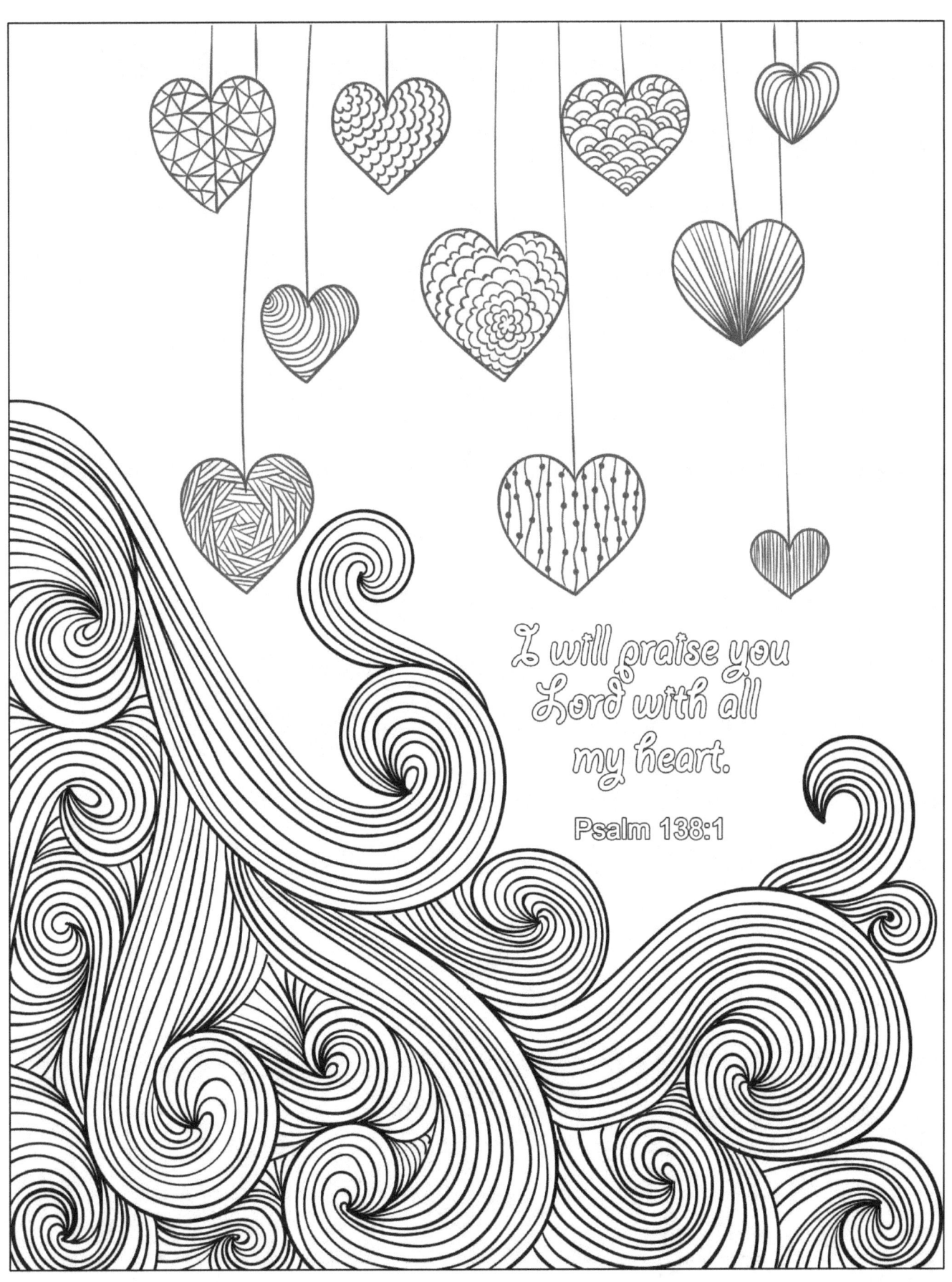

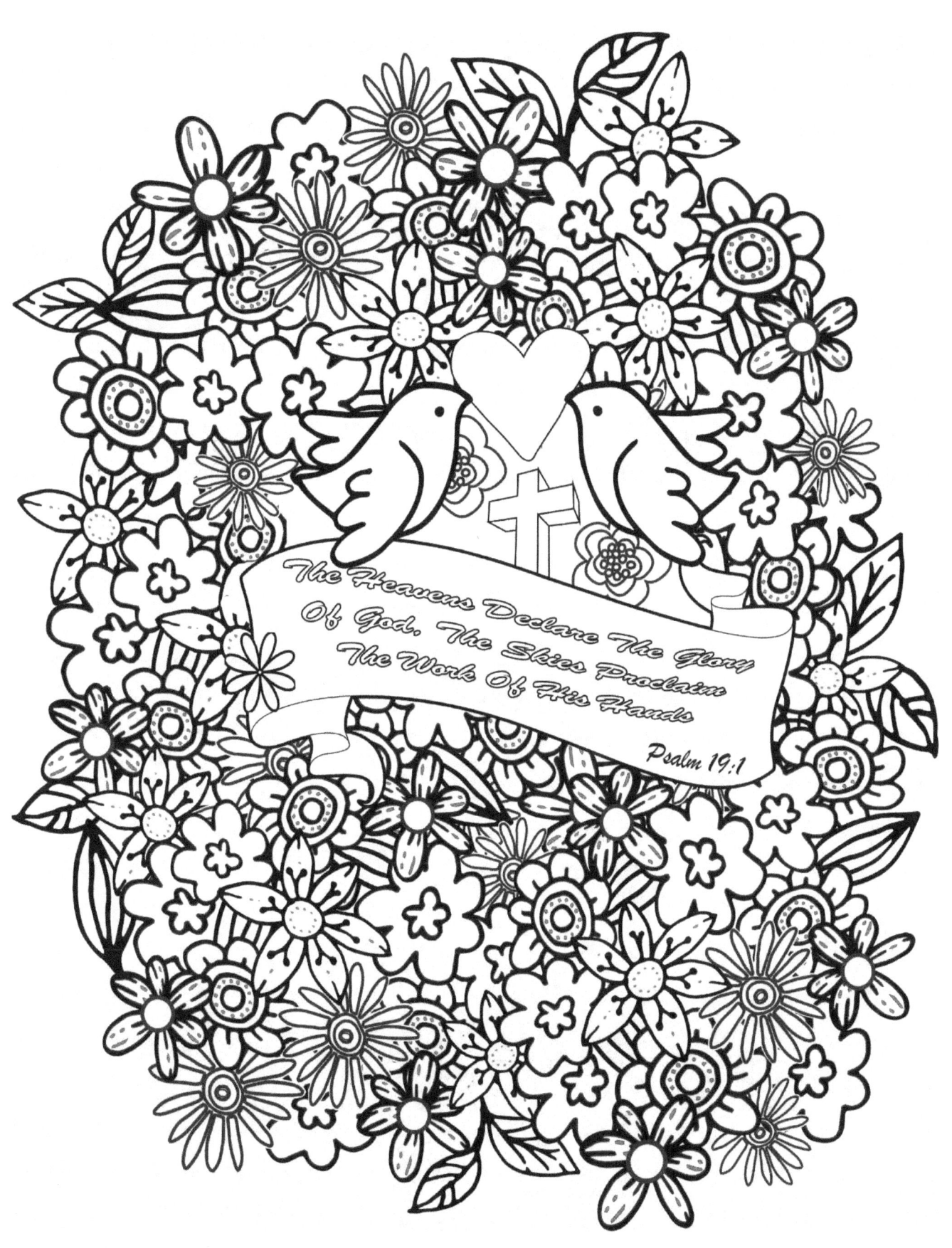

The Heavens Declare The Glory Of God, The Skies Proclaim The Work Of His Hands

Psalm 19:1

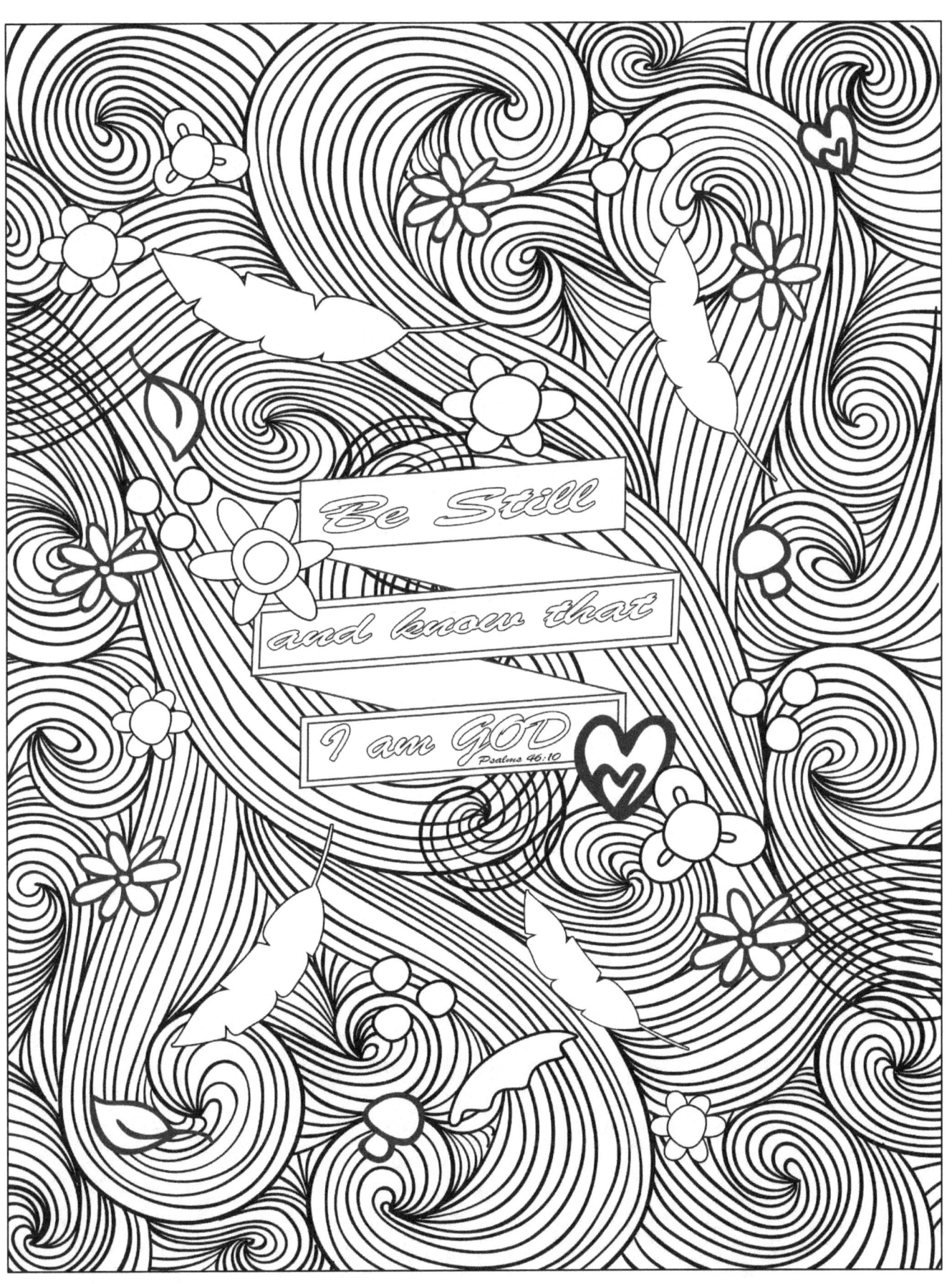

Be Still and know that I am GOD

Psalms 46:10

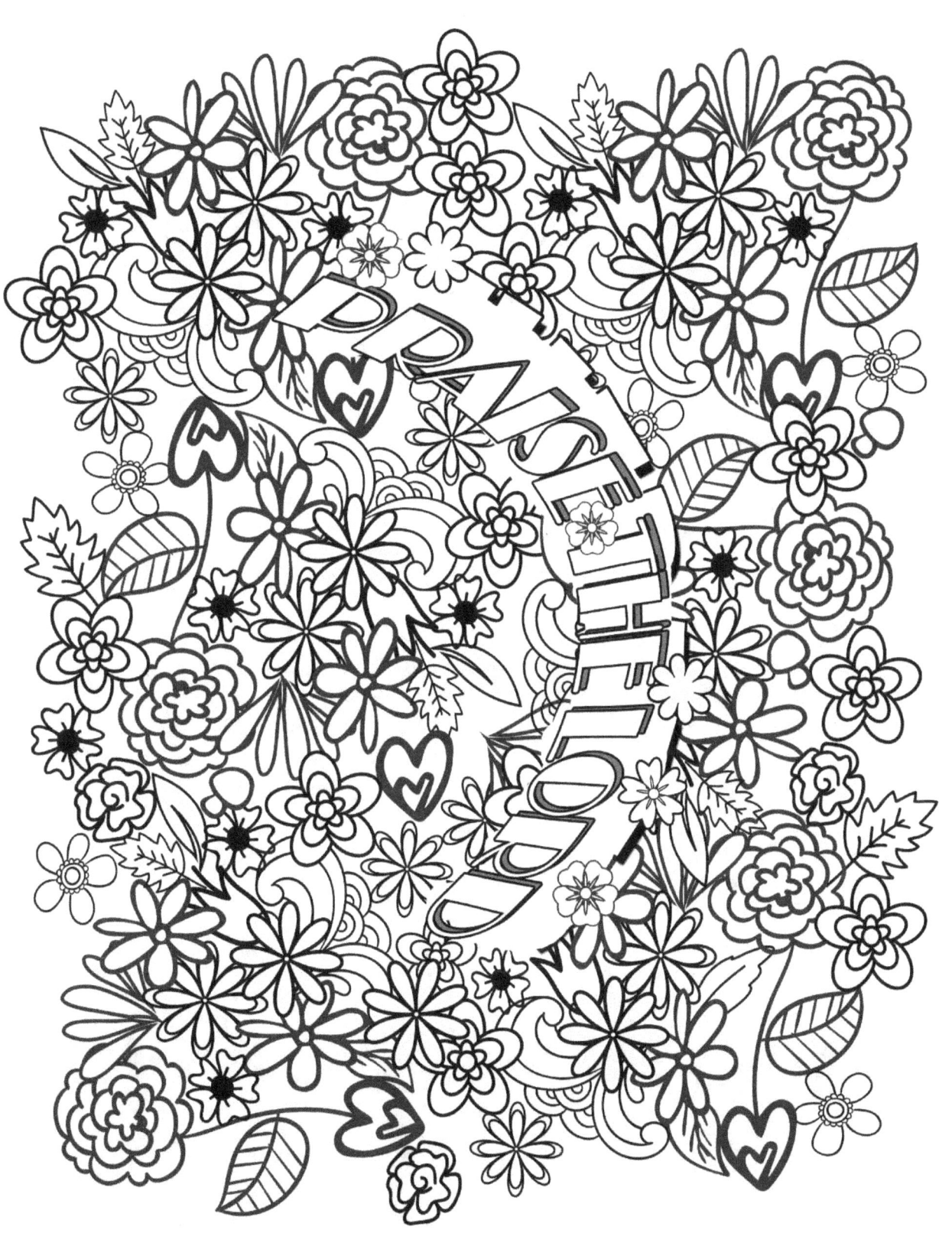

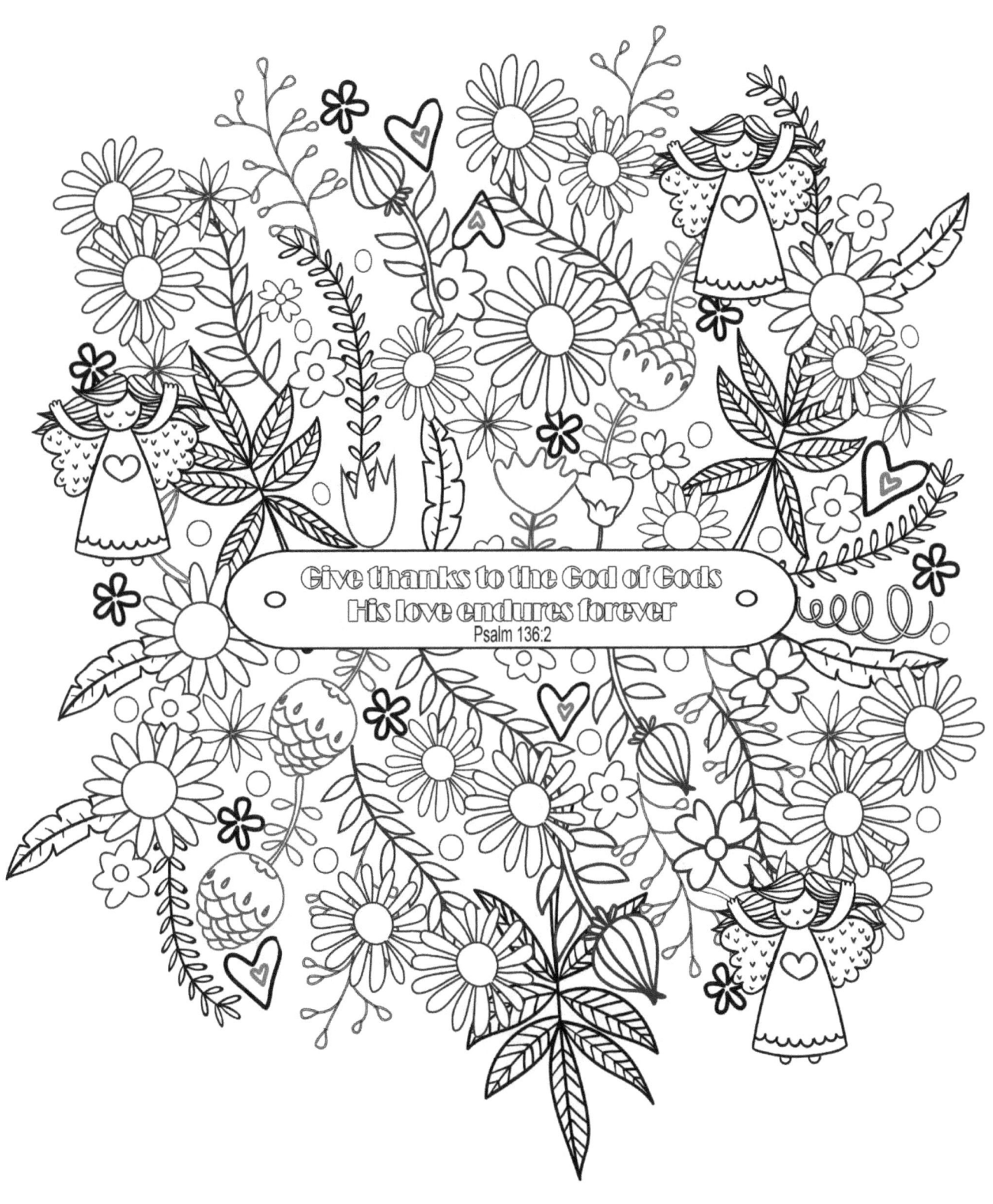

Give thanks to the God of Gods
His love endures forever
Psalm 136:2

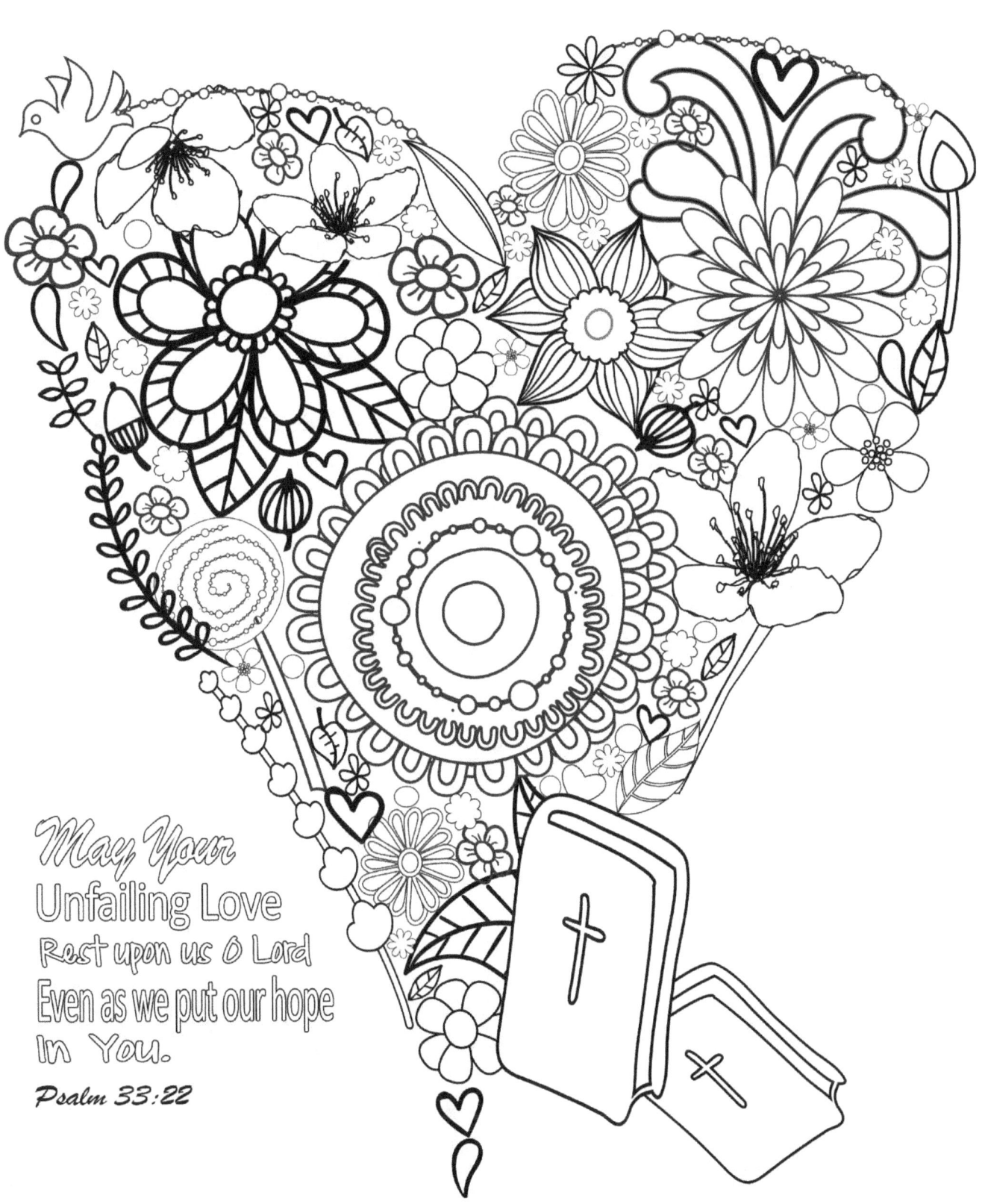

May Your
Unfailing Love
Rest upon us O Lord
Even as we put our hope
In You.

Psalm 33:22

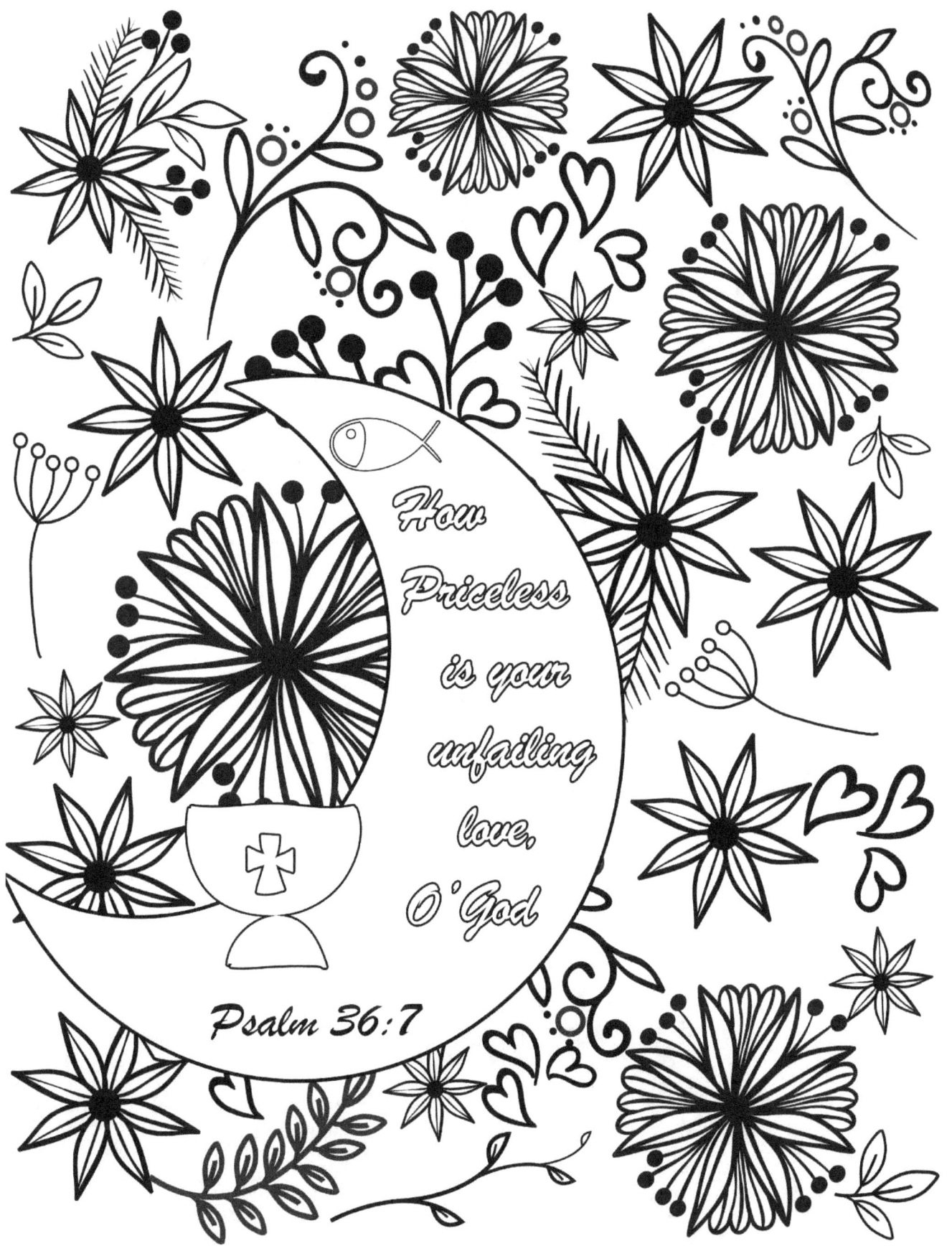

How Priceless is your unfailing love, O' God

Psalm 36:7

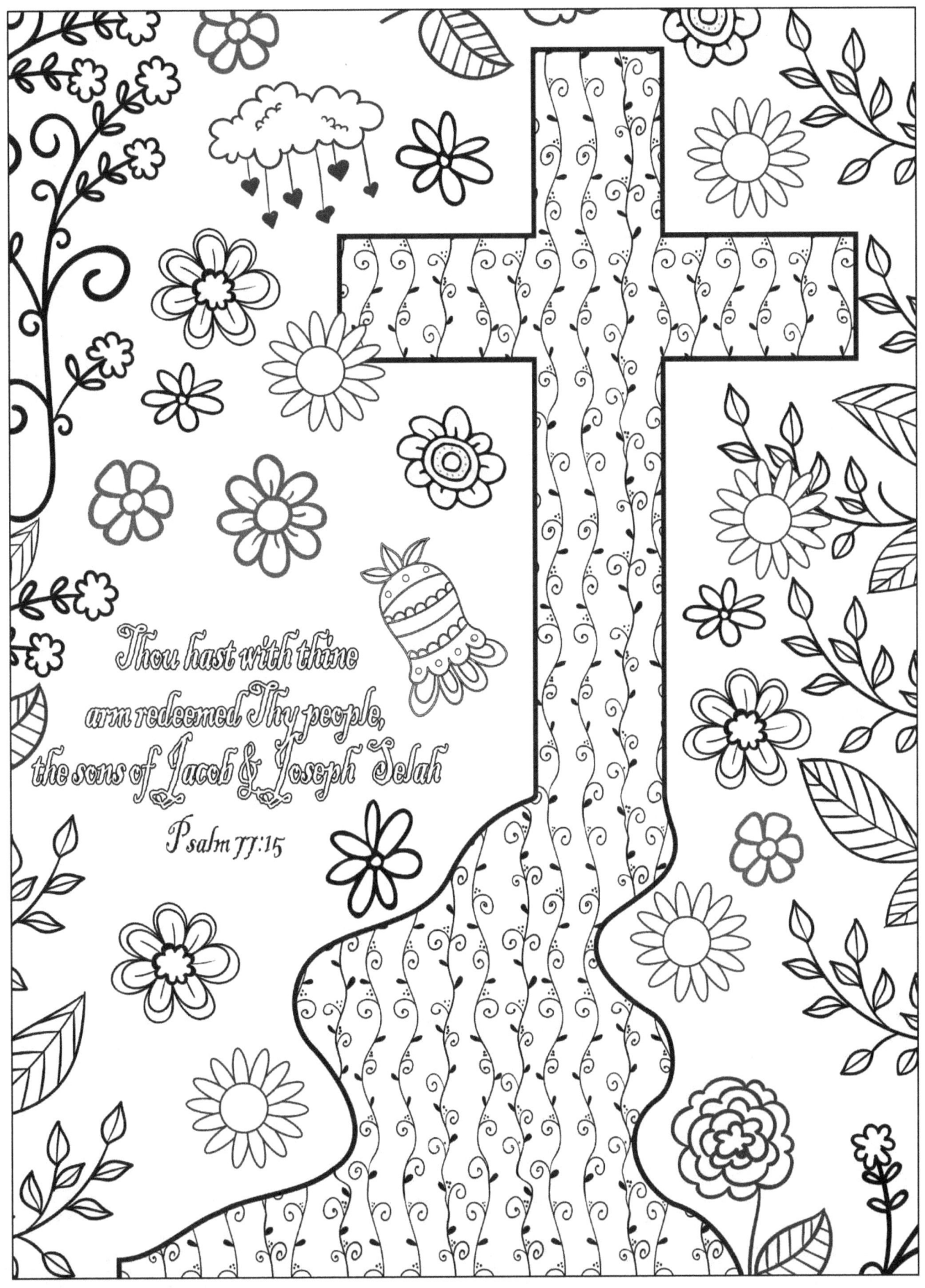

Thou hast with thine arm redeemed Thy people, the sons of Jacob & Joseph. Selah

Psalm 77:15

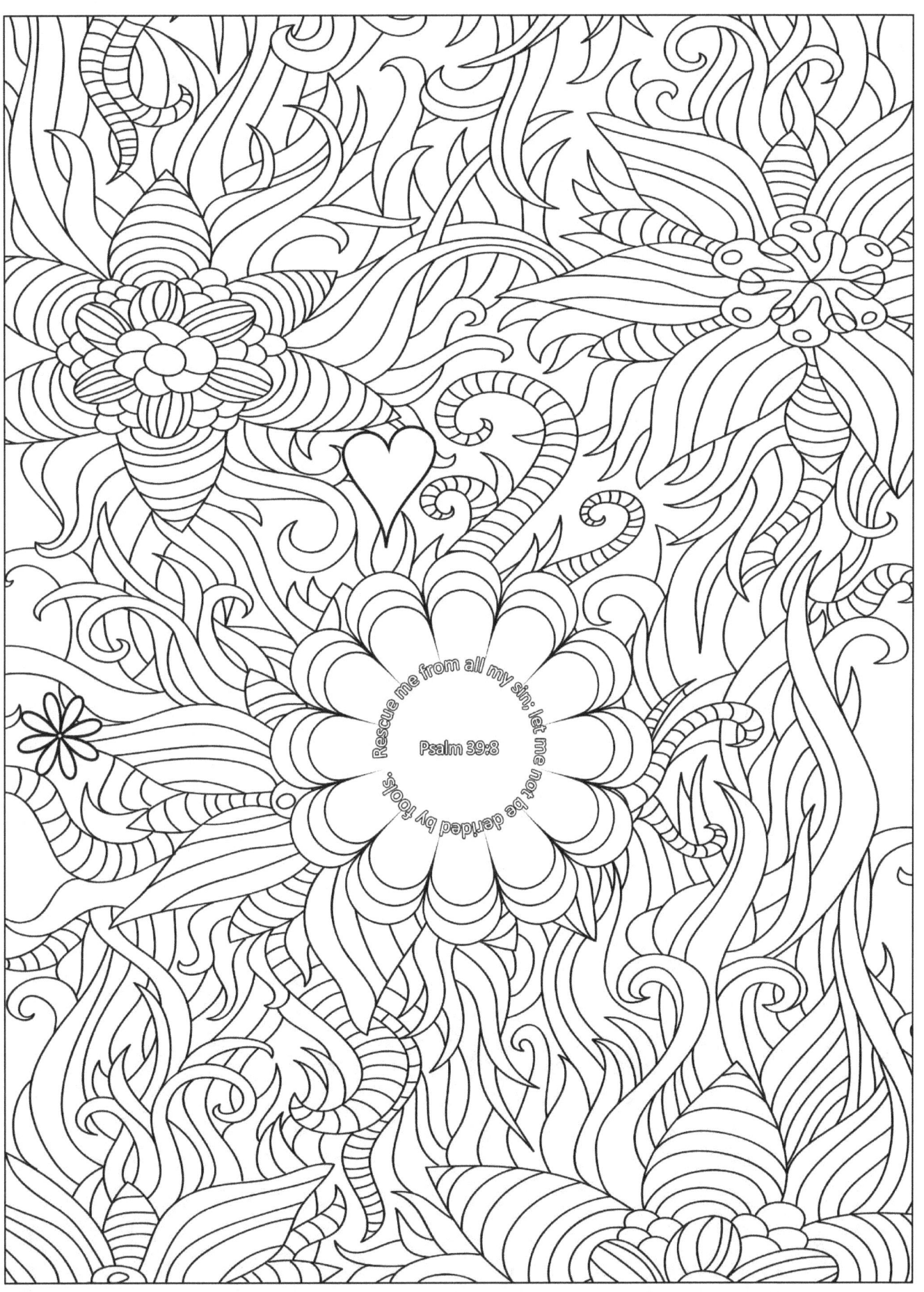

Rescue me from all my sin; let me not be derided by fools.

Psalm 39:8

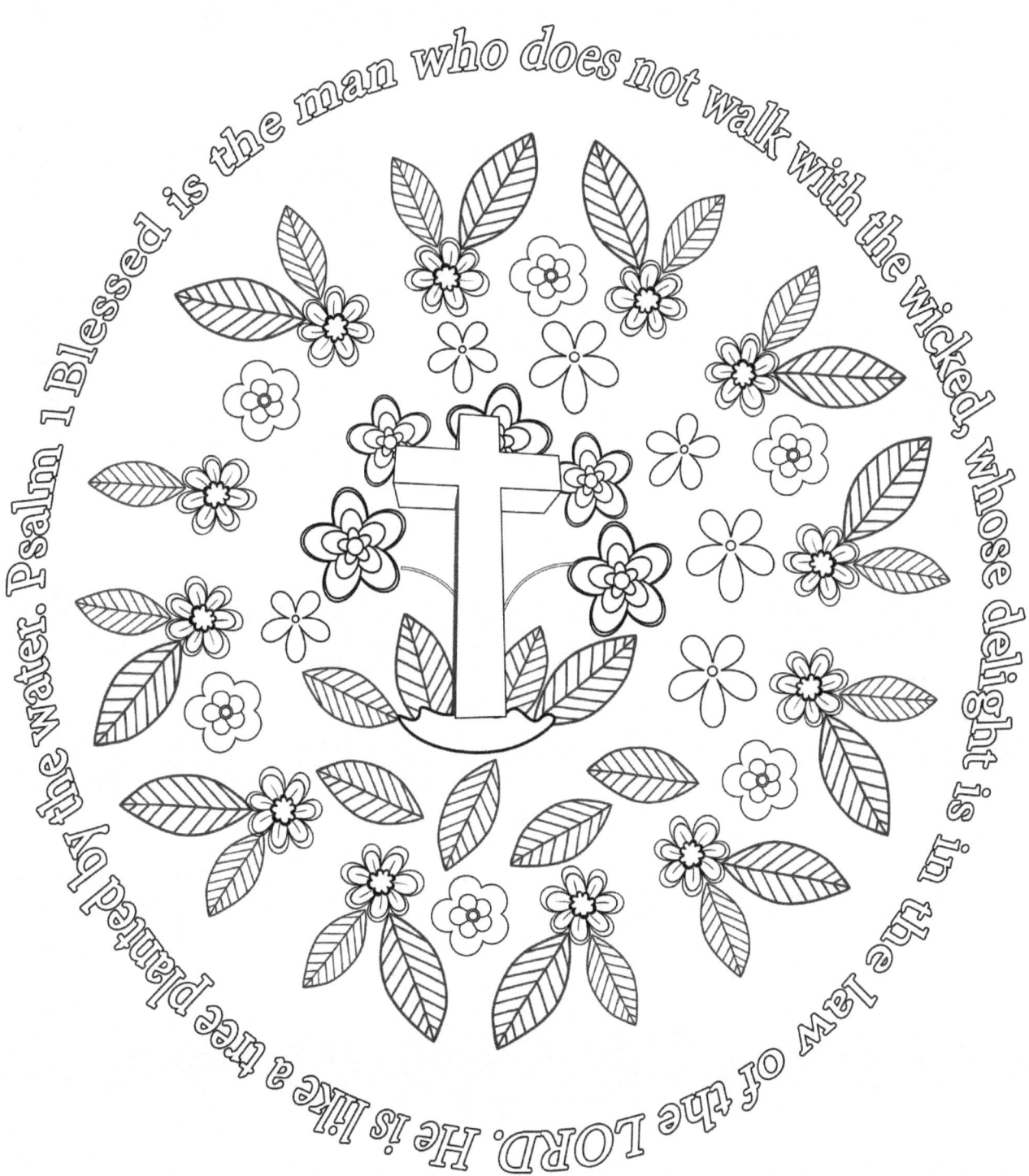

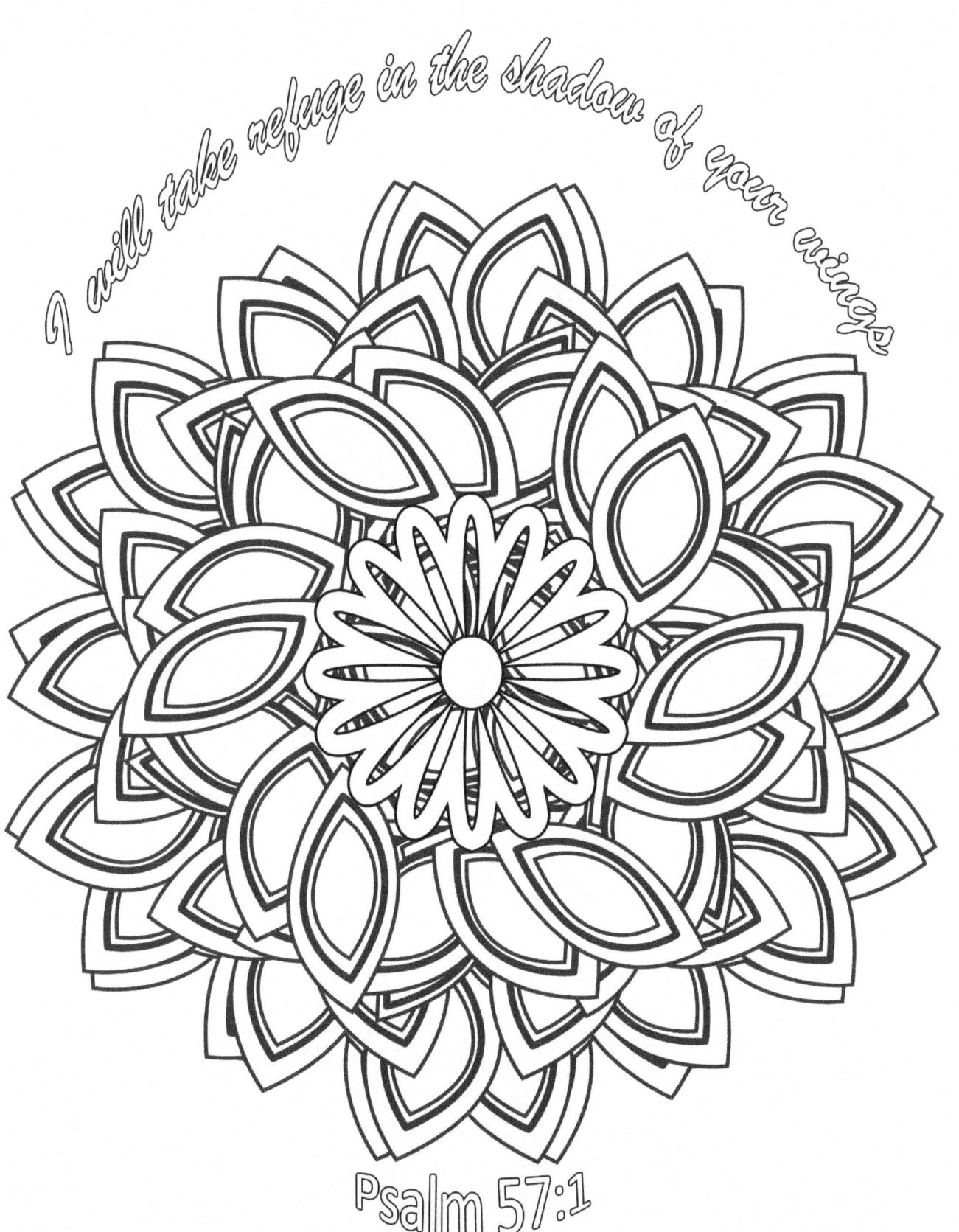

I will take refuge in the shadow of your wings

Psalm 57:1

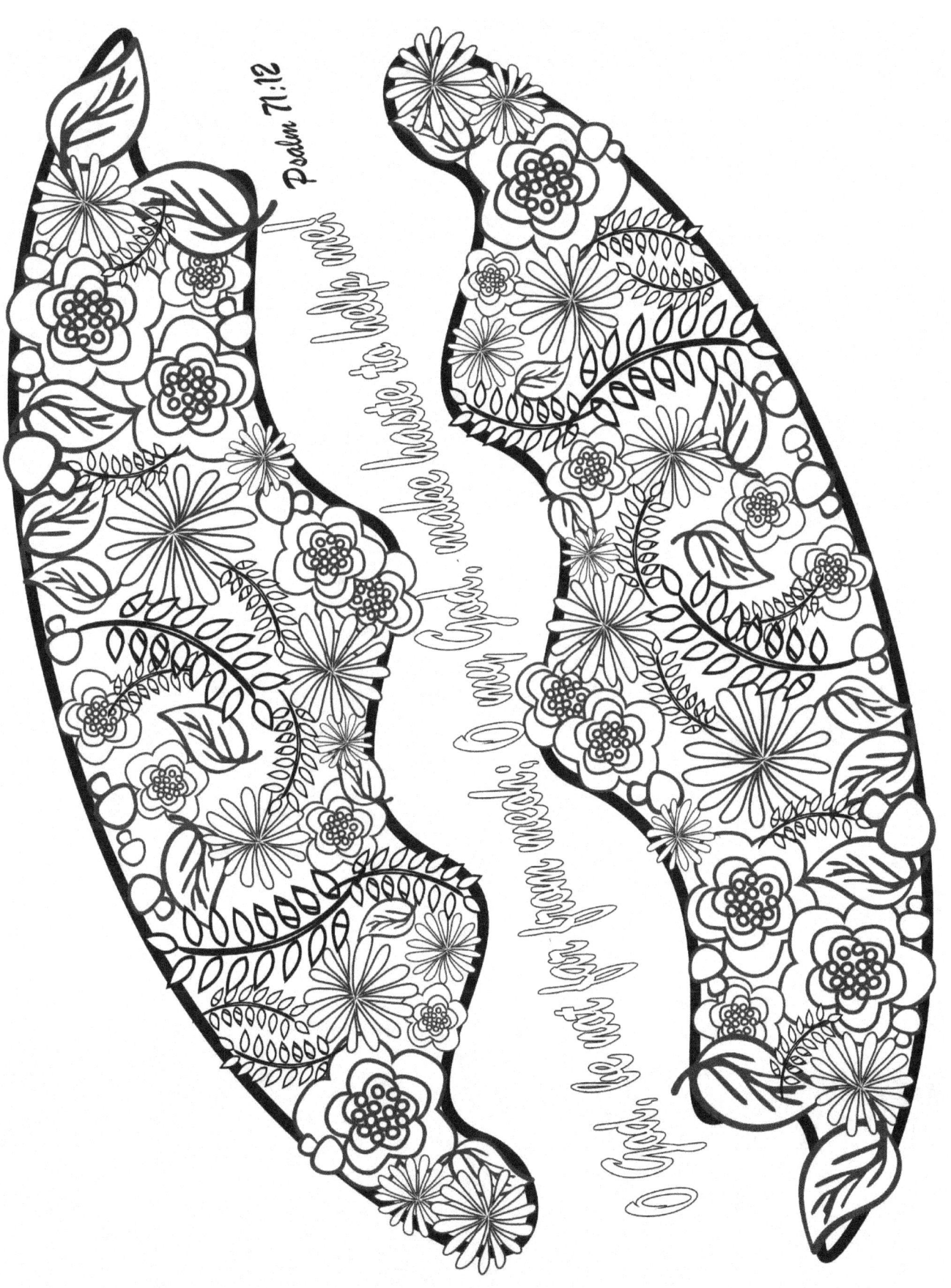

Psalm 71:12

O God, be not far from me! O my God, make haste to help me!

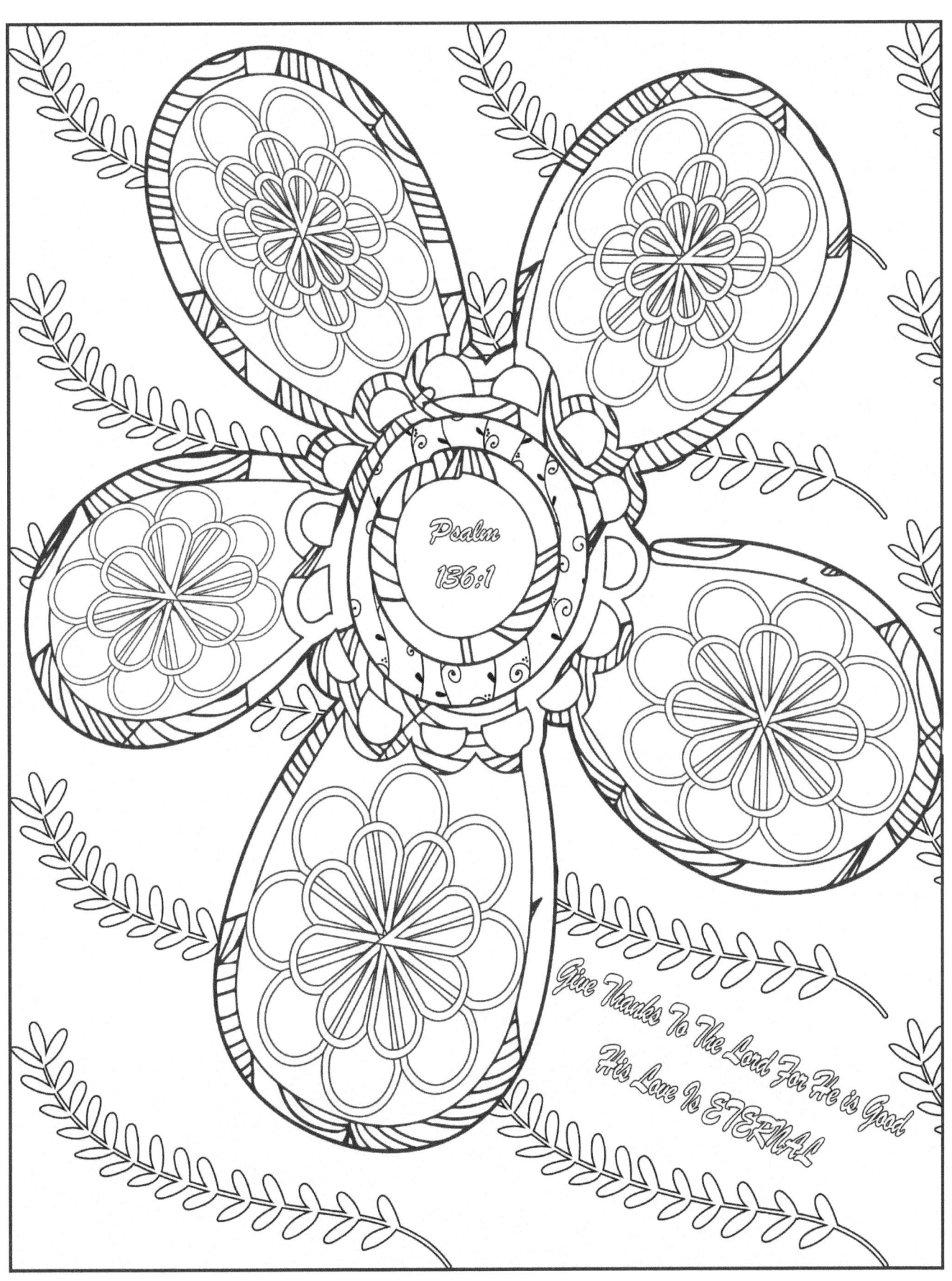

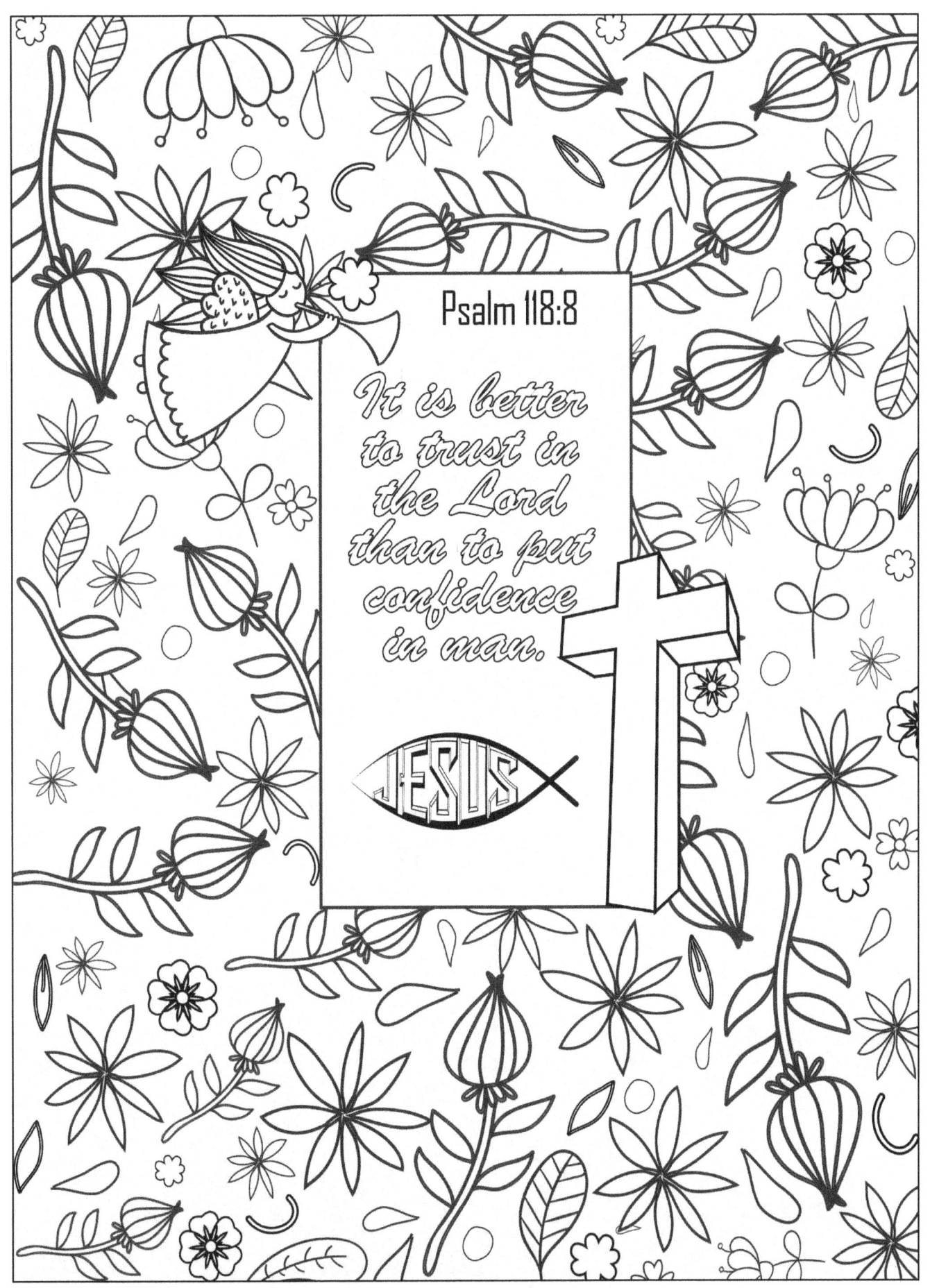

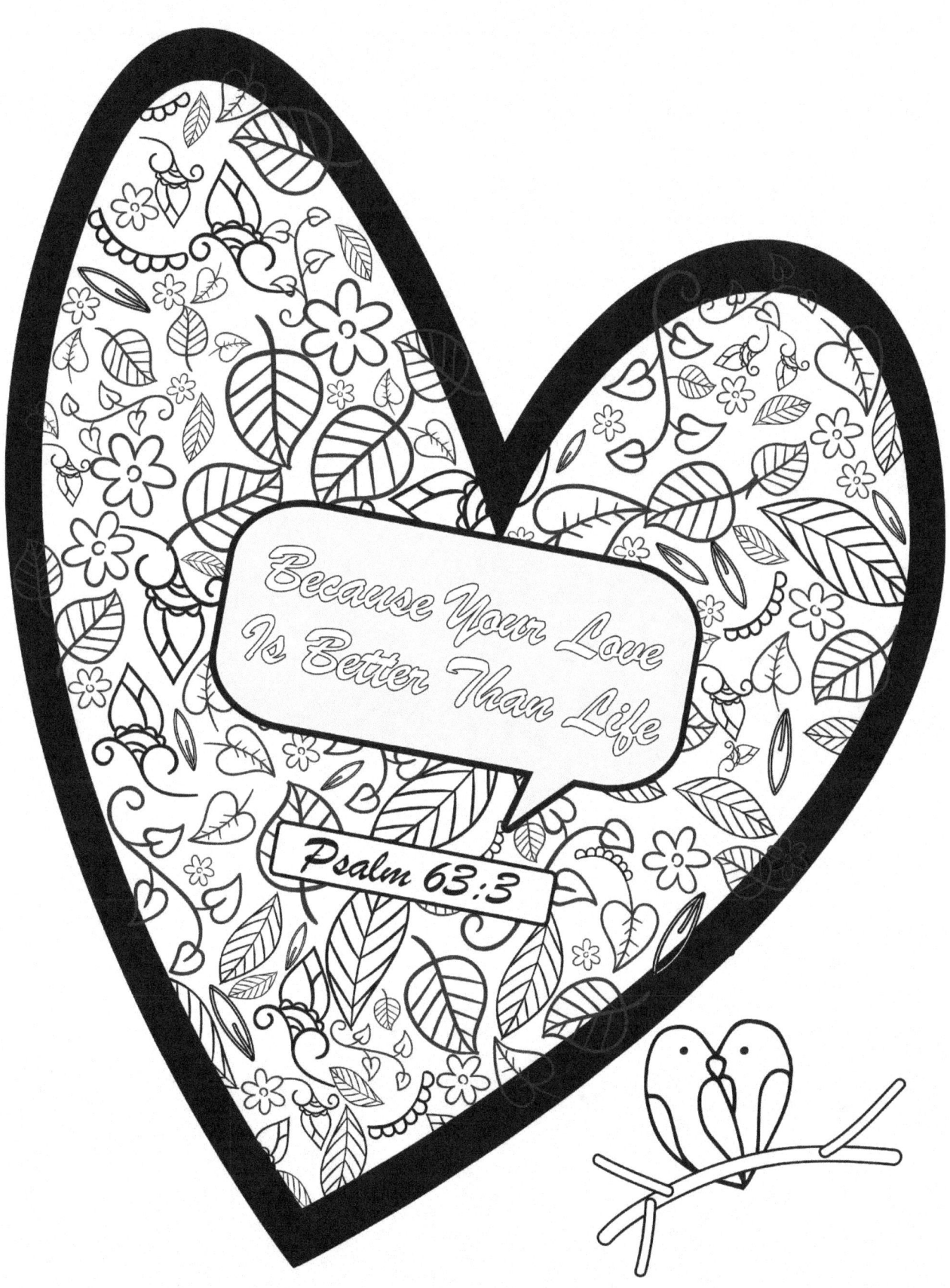

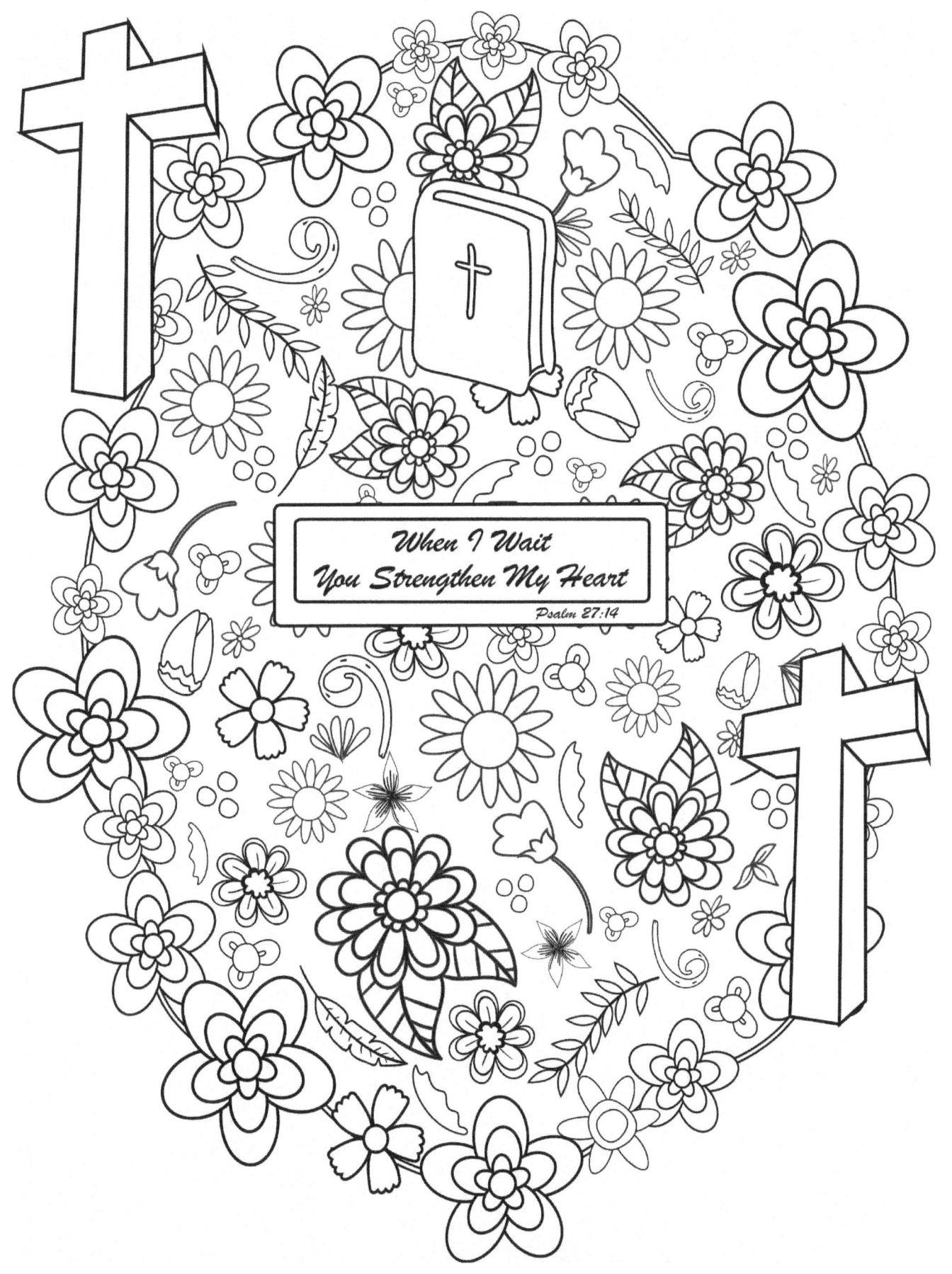

When I Wait
You Strengthen My Heart

Psalm 27:14

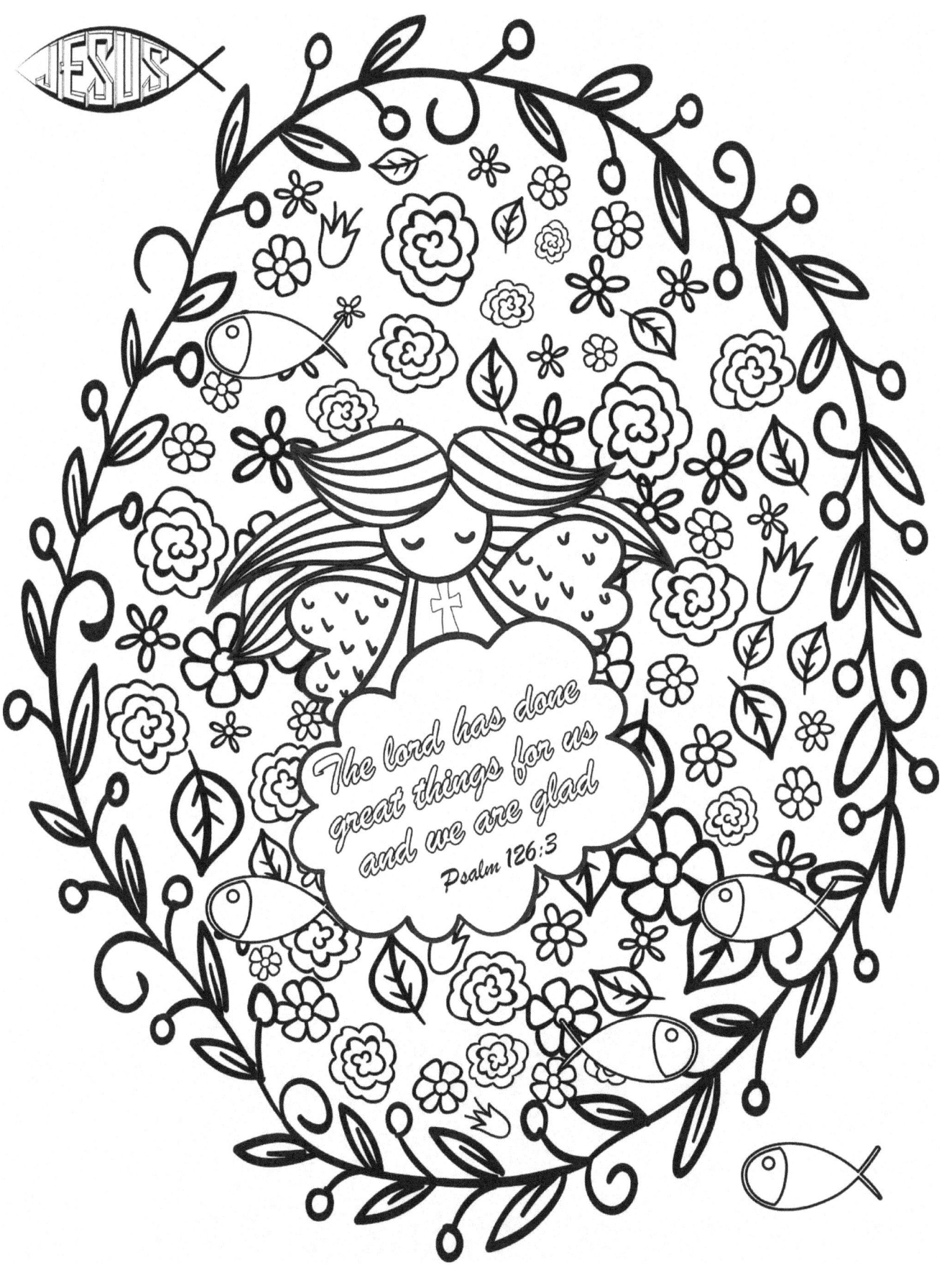

The lord has done great things for us and we are glad

Psalm 126:3

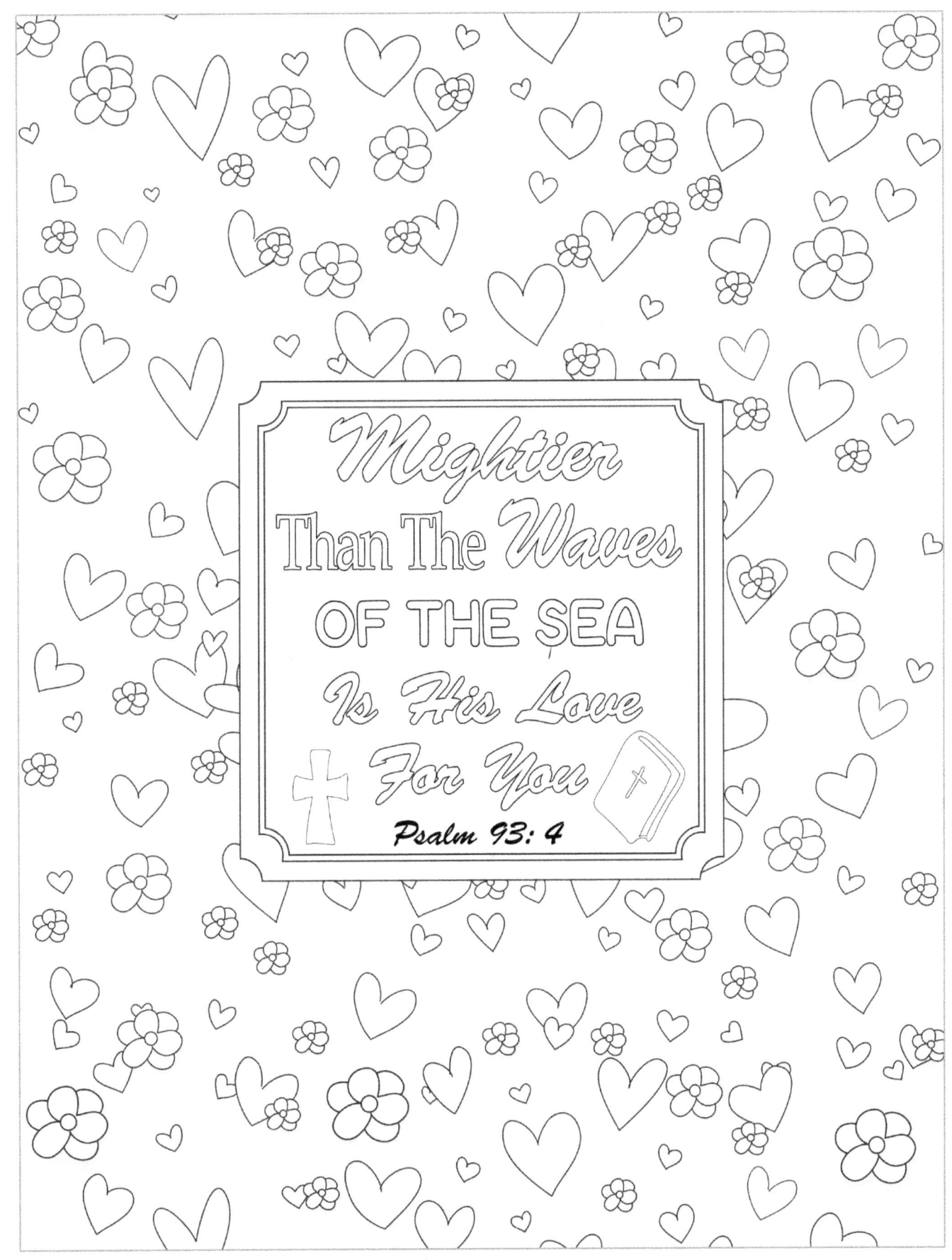

Mightier
Than The Waves
OF THE SEA
Is His Love
For You
Psalm 93: 4

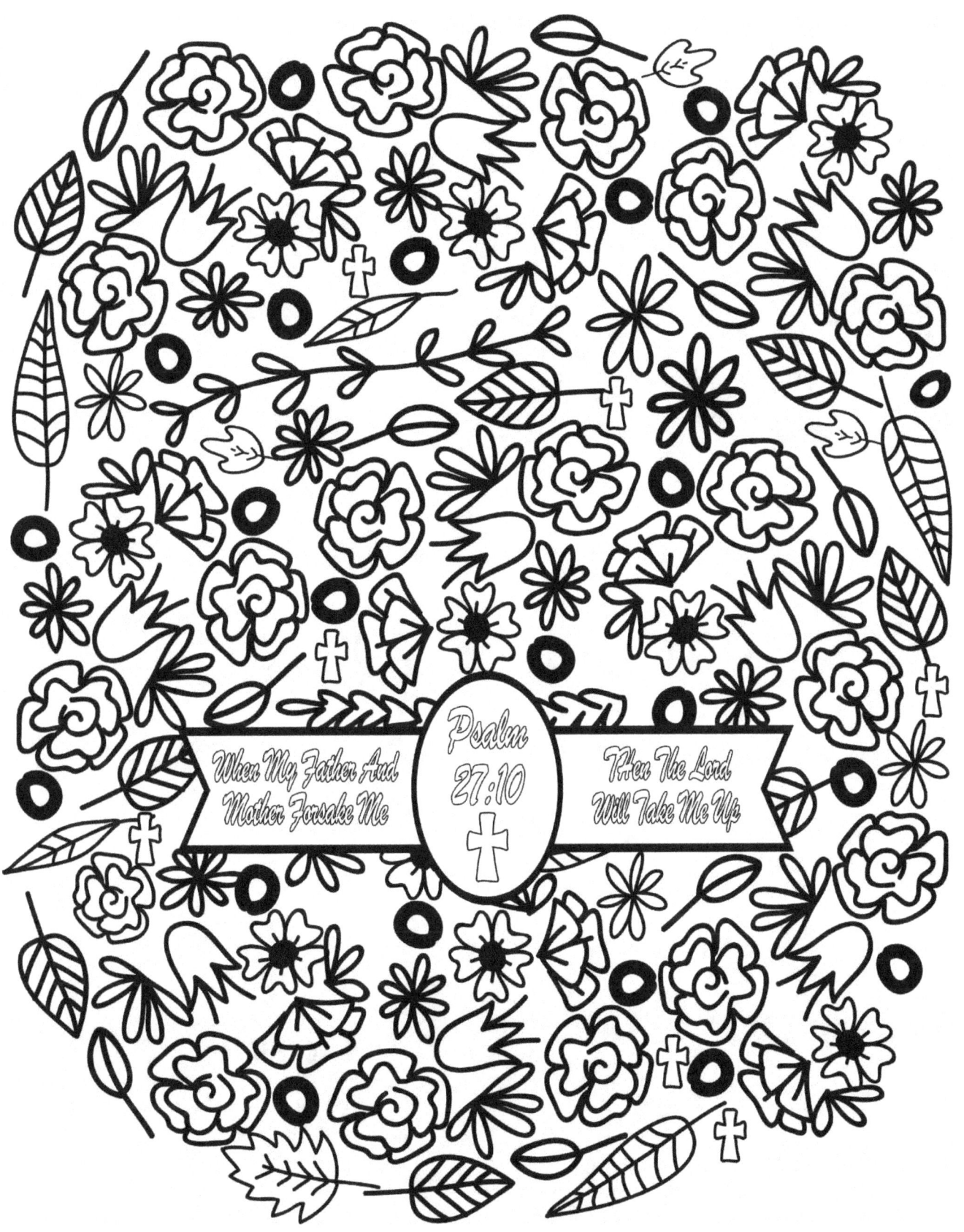

Psalm 27:10

When My Father And Mother Forsake Me

Then The Lord Will Take Me Up

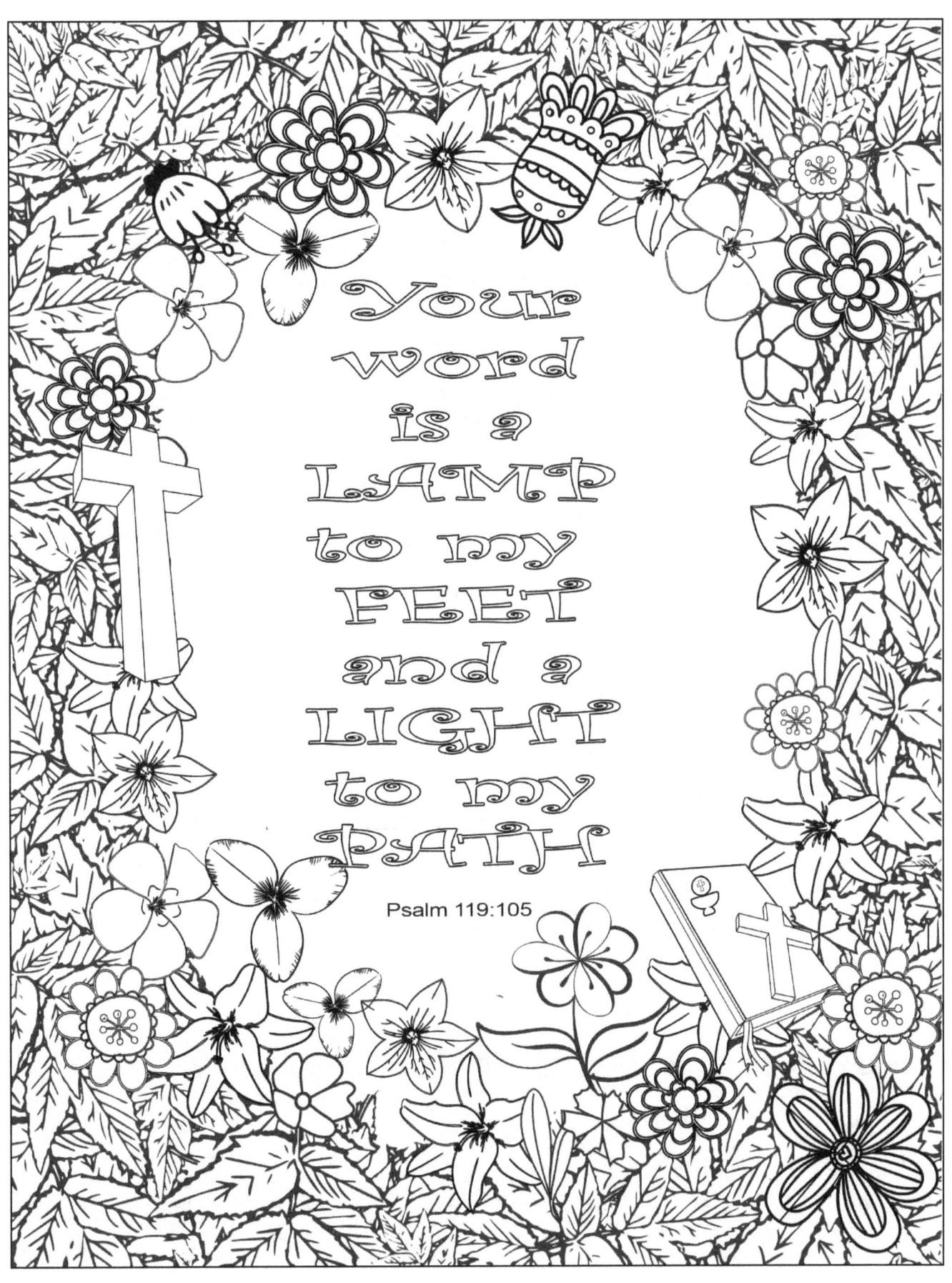

Your word is a LAMP to my FEET and a LIGHT to my PATH

Psalm 119:105

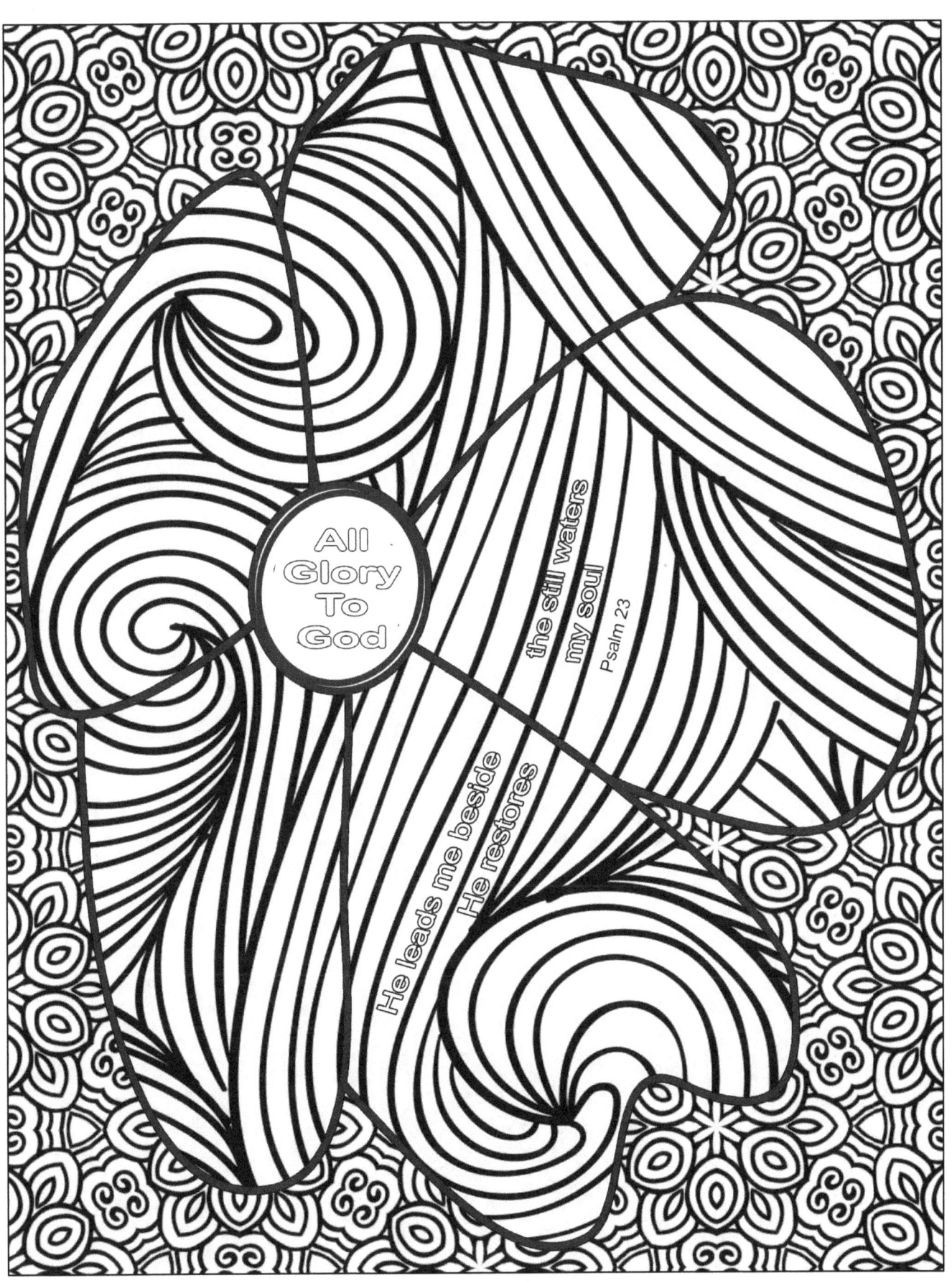

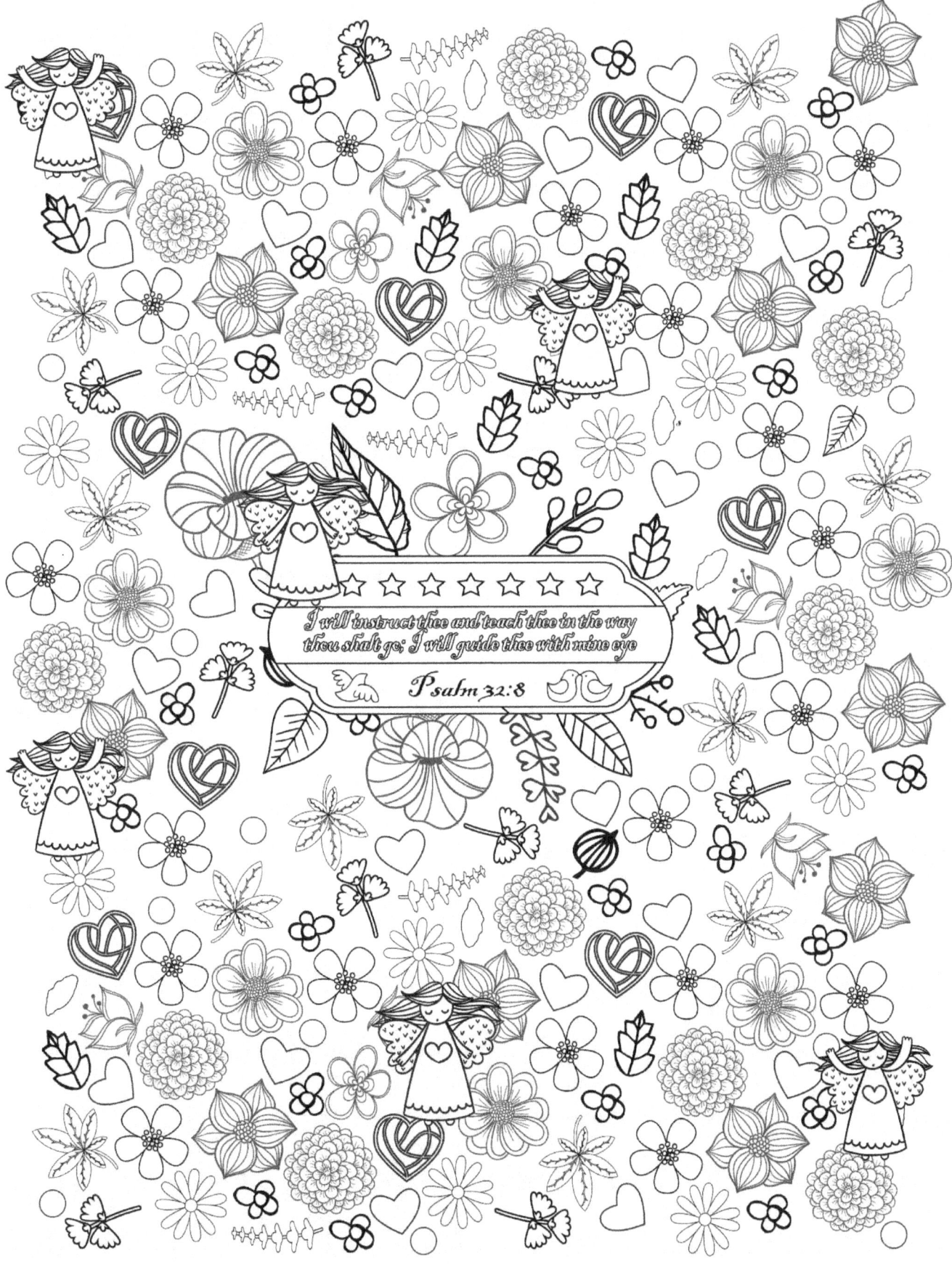

I will instruct thee and teach thee in the way thou shalt go; I will guide thee with mine eye

Psalm 32:8

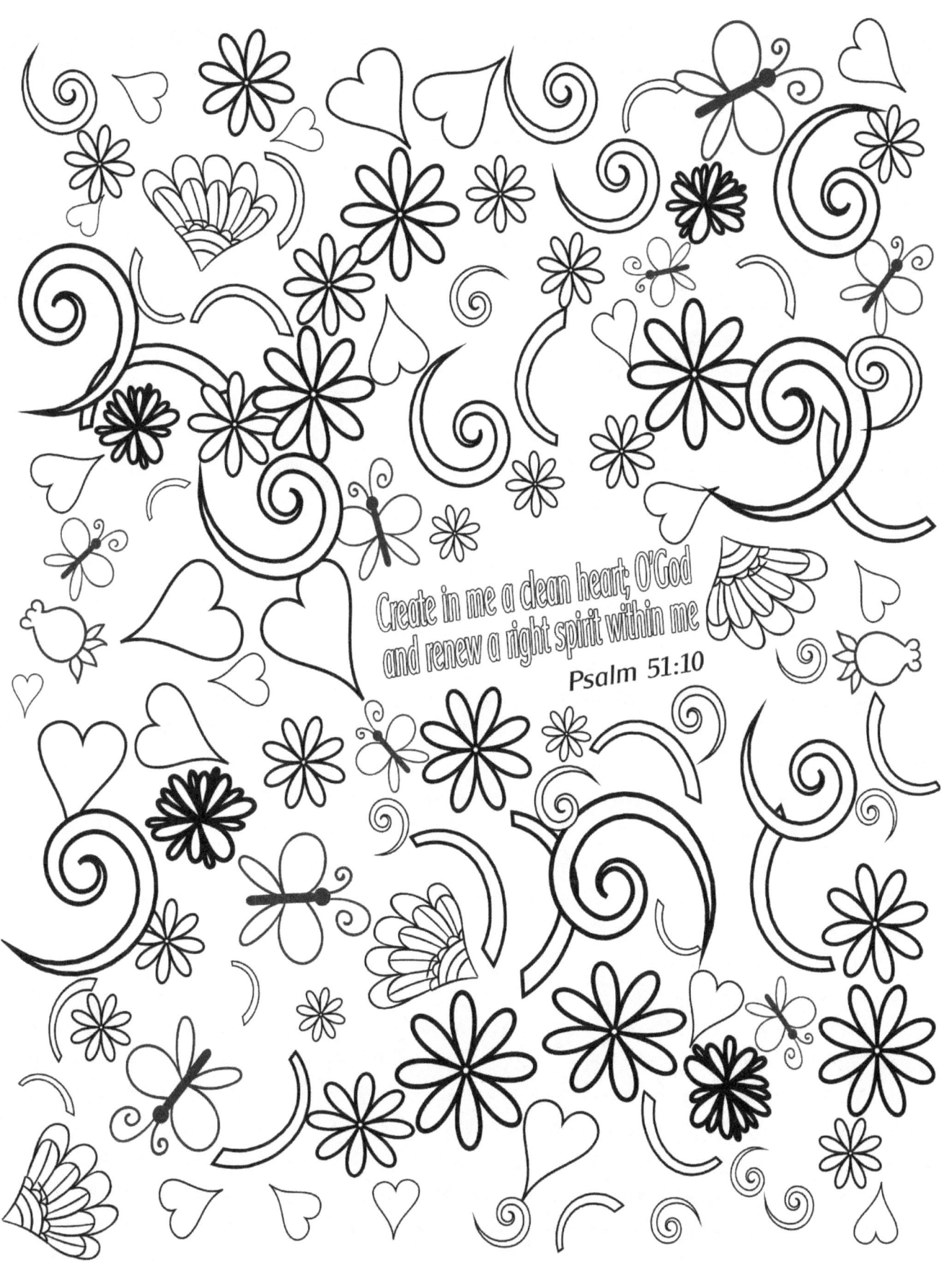

Create in me a clean heart; O'God and renew a right spirit within me

Psalm 51:10

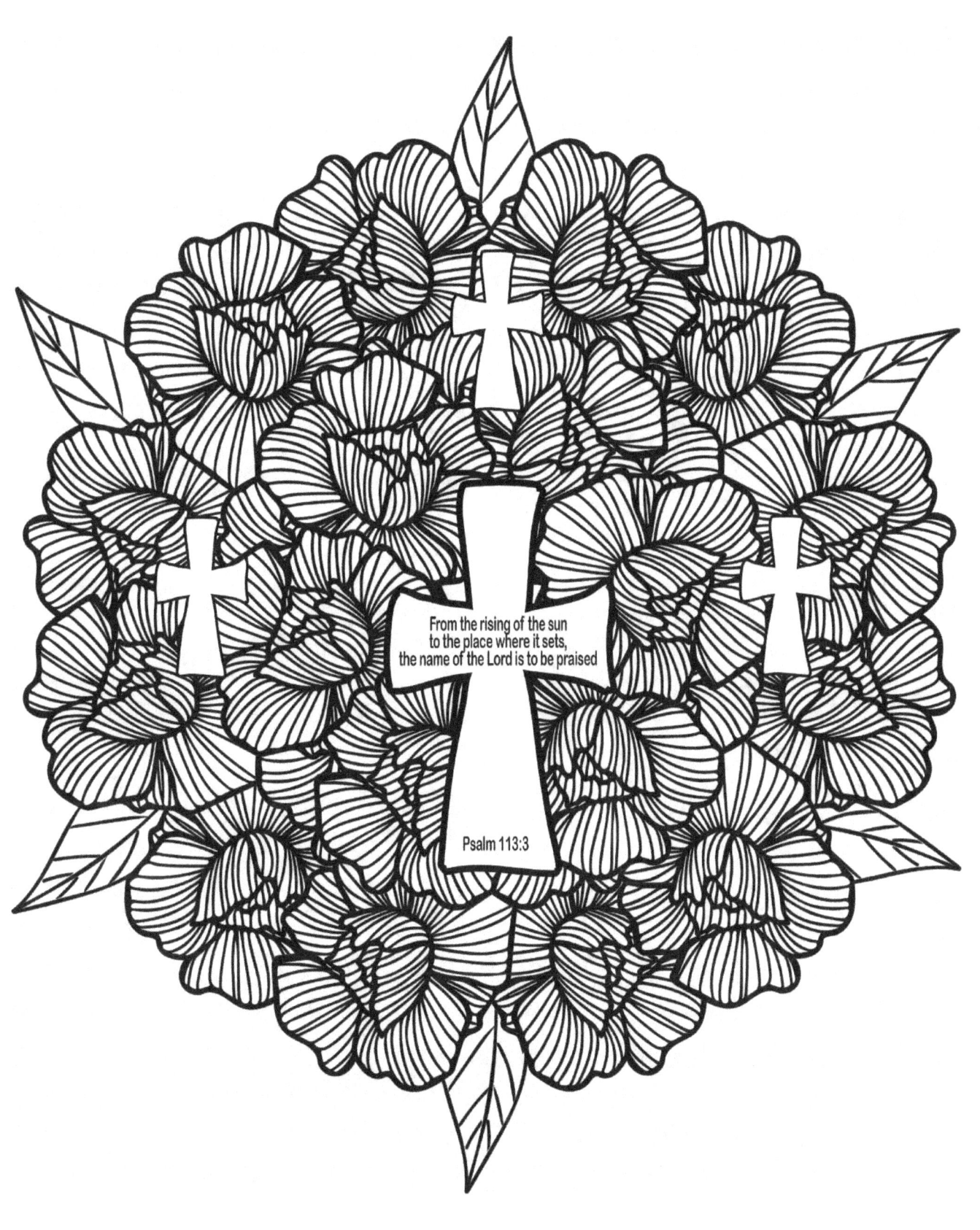

From the rising of the sun
to the place where it sets,
the name of the Lord is to be praised

Psalm 113:3

www.ingramcontent.com/pod-product-compliance
Lightning Source LLC
Chambersburg PA
CBHW081250180526
45170CB00007B/2360